A Primer of Hinduism

By

D. S. SARMA, M.A.

Sri Ramakrishna Math
Mylapore Madras 600 004

Published by
The President
Sri Ramakrishna Math
Mylapore, Chennai-4

IX-2M 2C-1-2003
ISBN 81-7120-444-9

Printed in India at
Sri Ramakrishna Math Printing Press
Mylapore, Chennai-4

CONTENTS

EXTRACTS FROM PREFACE TO THE FIRST EDITION (1929)

When, three or four years ago, I began to write this Primer in the form of questions and answers for the benefit of my children, I little dreamt that I should one day have to write the Preface to it in the mood in which I am writing it to-day. For the light of my heart and of my home, the dear one of whose marvellously precocious intelligence I dared not speak even to my friends, lest they should disbelieve me or the Gods should be jealous, has now been taken away from me. A void has been created in my family which can never be filled. The only consolation that is left to me now is that which I found on that fatal day, when, after everything was over and done—dust to dust, ashes to ashes, and soul to Soul—I turned in my anguish to the Gītā and read in the first verse that met my eye:—

"I am Death that devours all; and I am the Source of all things to be."

The reader will now understand the significance of the dialogue form in the following pages. The work was originally undertaken for the illumination of her who now figures in it as an interlocutor. Later on, as it developed in my hands, it was published in parts in the Presidency College Magazine as a conversation between two fictitious characters—a teacher and a pupil. The articles attracted some attention, and I received several letters from unknown correspondents asking me to proceed with the exposition and to publish the parts together in the form of a book. In meeting their wishes I have considerably expanded the dialogue and restored the original interlocutors, as I desired that the book should ever be associated with the dear one for whom it was primarily intended.

As this Primer tries to provide a common platform for all classes and sects, and as it tries to deal with religion not in a technical manner but in close connection with life and conduct, I hope that all those who are interested in the introduction of religious education in our schools and colleges will give it a fair trial.

D.S. SARMA

PUBLISHER'S NOTE

The Primer of Hinduism was first published by Prof. D.S. Sarma five decades back. It was reprinted by the Vivekananda College, Madras, of which Prof. Sarma was the first Principal. Originally he wrote it for the instruction of his own children, as he points out in his Preface, and he used it afterwards for the religion class of the students of the colleges where he worked as a Professor. We are now bringing out a new edition of it with an Introduction and selection of representative scriptural passages, in order that this worthy book may be brought to the notice of a wider public.

Prof. D.S. Sarma was a well-known educationist and teacher of English in the first half of the century. But side by side he was also a very lucid and learned exponent of Hindu religion and philosophy, having contributed several articles and books and delivered numerous lectures expounding this theme. Many of these are bound to survive, but the writing that deserves most to be preserved for posterity is the present publication.

There are very few brief and comprehensive expositions of the universal tenets of Hinduism available today, and so Prof. Srama's book is to be welcomed as ably fulfilling the need in this respect. Both the modern Hindu who is brought up in an un-Hindu environment, and the followers of other faiths who want an authentic exposition of Hinduism is a short compass, would find this to be the book most helpful to satisfy their need.

While the author calls the book a Primer, it is much more than that. It touches briefly on all the fundamental doctrines of Hindu religion and philosophy, and can very well form the basis of a detailed exposition of it suited to the needs of students at different levels of understanding.

To the original book of Prof. Sarma we have added as Introduction, a general article of Hinduism, and as an Appendix, a representative selection of passages from the Hindu scriptures having a bearing on the fundamental verities of religion.

Ramakrishna Math, Publisher
Madras.
July 1981

INTRODUCTION

I HINDUISM, BRAHMANISM OR VEDANTA—WHICH?

An exposition of Hinduism, either in its primary or detailed form, is far more difficult than that of other great world religions. Being the oldest of all religions, and being also the end product of a long process of interaction of various cultures, creeds and cults in the crucible of time, it has gained a complexity, a width and a depth, which other religions do not have. A religion devoid of a founder, or a date of origin, or any definite creed; noted for a plethora of scriptures, deities and rituals; practising an attitude of tolerance for all kinds of cults based on bewildering mythologies; possessing no authorised church or priesthood to interpret or enforce its practices and teachings—Hinduism presents a chaotic appearance, which makes the task of an interpreter very formidable. It is true of all religions that it is only one born and brought up in it who can get an insight into its structure and tenets. In the case of Hinduism this is all the more so. A religion is a simple lived experience for a participant, but for an exponent it becomes a conceptualised something, analysable into parts and presentable for an objective study. With all the imperfections of this approach, that is the only way in which a religion can be studied and interpreted.

We shall not in this Introduction attempt to expound the principal teachings of Hinduism, as it has been ably done by the author of this Primer. Though he calls it a Primer, it is much more than that, as all aspects of Hinduism have been touched upon by him in a very compact and clear manner in the text. We shall therefore confine ourselves to some of its important features. Hinduism consists in fact of several religions or cults having their own conceptions of the Deity, traditions and practices, but endowed with a unity like that of a bouquet of flowers, brought about by the winding strings of certain philosophical ideas and a world view common to them all. In times past it was closely but wrongly bound to a social organisation known as caste system, in which birth was the basis for determining the status of individuals. But the birth-based caste is entirely different from the Varnashrama system which is upheld by the Vedic tradition. For, in the true Varnashrama, a man's worth is determined not by birth but by his Guna—the dominance of one or the other of the well-known aspects of Prakriti, Sattva, Rajas and Tamas, and the way of life he follows as a result of such dominance. Whether such a non-exploiting and non-competitive social system entirely based on one's fitness to serve the body politic was ever actually practised in historical times, is doubtful. But it is true that at some stage of its development, what is called Hinduism today came to be identified with a caste-based social system that was wrongly called Varnashrama Dharma. Consequently it has become a popular fashion in the study of comparative religion to say that a Hindu is born so and not made, meaning that Hinduism is an ethnic religion and not a universal one accomodating all who want to participate in its spiritual ministration.

In the past all the great Acharyas, the teachers of the Vedic religion, used to interpret it as intrinsically related to the Varnashrama social system. While it is undeniable that a non-exploiting and non-competitive society is immensely helpful in focussing man's mind on spiritual ideas, any association of it with a birth-based caste system is obnoxious to the mind of man in this non-feudal age. Modern critics of Hinduism have therefore sarcastically termed it as Brahmanism. But this has been countered by the new authoritative interpretation of it given by Swami Vivekananda at the turn of the last century. Swami Vivekananda has interpreted Hinduism in its doctrinal form, dissecting it away from its old social context and termed it as Vedantism in contrast to the sarcastic name of Brahmanism, with which persons who wanted to downgrade and ridicule the Vedic religion preferred to call it. Taken out of its social context, Hinduism or Vedantism gives man a world view based on certain philosohical notions, and freedom to select for his daily practice any of the personality-based cults originating in India or outside. Thus Vedantism is remarkable for both its breadth as well as its depth.

II THE THEORY OF SAMSARA AND MOKSHA

The principal feature of Vedantism and its first tenet is the cyclic view of Time and man's involvement in it. What is man? Whence has he come? What is he here for? These are the ever-recurring questions that tease the human mind. The answers given are that man is a Spirit, a spark of the Sat-chit-ananda, endowed with a body-mind and undergoing a recurring process of births and deaths, caught as he is in the cyclic movement of Time. This state is called Samsara, the repetitive process of life and death. There is no beginning for it, as its framework of Time is cyclic in movement. Matter (Prakriti) and souls (Jivas) are not created at any moment of Time, but are eternally present as dependent existences or as the body of the Supreme Being. They are sometimes described as the two aspects of the Power or Sakti of God under the names of Maya-Sakti and Jiva-Sakti of the Sat-chit-ananda. They come into manifestation at the beginning of a cycle of Time, and at the end dissolve in Him, remaining in their causal conditions, only to come into manifestation again when the new cycle of Time starts after the earlier dissolution.

The Jiva undergoes countless embodiments until he evolves his inherent perfection as the Spirit. In Samsara, owing to the encrustation of Karma or tendencies accrued in earlier lives through one's own actions, that inherent divinity is shrunk and hidden, but never effaced or destroyed. The purpose of the creative cycle is to elicit this divine potentiality of the Spirit and bring it into higher and higher states of perfection. These repeated embodiments are the result of Karma or action in the earlier phases of the Jiva's involvement in Samsara. All actions done leave some tendencies on the mind, and also entitlement for enjoyments or suffering according to the nature of those actions. The accumulation of these effects acquired in births past is the Karma potential regulating the embodiments and experiences of the Jivas. This theory is essential for a conception of a just and righteous God. For, any theory accepting a first creation will have to attribute the responsibility for all suffering and evil to God. In the cyclic theory of creation, there is no first creation and hence no beginning for the Jiva. Therefore it has to be accepted that an original quantum of Karma goes with the very conception of Jiva, and to ask for a beginning for it is only to beg the question.

The Jiva's entanglement in Samsara therefore means this association with a body-mind in repeated life-spans here or in other worlds, regulated by Karma which is of his own making. In these repeated embodiments he passes through innumerable bodies of different species of beings. He might have passed through the bodies of animal creations; he might have found several embodiments among the humans and the Devas, all according to the nature of his Karma. It is in human life alone that he acquires good and bad Karmas. In other kinds of embodiments he undergoes sufferings or enjoyments to which he is eligible by his Karma. If he has perpetrated heinous sins, he may degenerate into animal body also. If he has a preponderance of highly meritorious Karma, entitling him to enjoyments of a very refined nature, he gets embodiment in Indra's heaven. If the Karma of the Jiva is predominantly sinful, he will even have to undergo the sufferings of purgatory to atone for his sins. When he has exhausted his preponderating meritorious or sinful Karma as the case may be, he is born again as man and undergoes enjoyments and sufferings for his residuary Karma. What is more, it is only in this human birth that the Jiva gets an opportunity to acquire new Karma through good and bad actions, as also to overcome the bondage of Karma as a whole and attain Mukti or liberation through devotion and knowledge (Bhakti and Jnana).

So, human birth is of supreme importance. It is the only embodiment in which the Jiva can evolve into greater and greater perfections as also acquire merits entitling him to heavenly enjoyments. The ultimate values which a Jiva can have in life here and hereafter are stated to be Dharma (moral worth), Artha (wealth and power), Kama (enjoyments), and Moksha (liberation), of which Dharma and Moksha can be had only in human birth. Dharma includes all the meritorious actions that yield heavenly enjoyments and also the virtues that go for the refinement of human nature. Moksha is the highest value, consisting as it does in release from the enjoyments and sufferings of repeated births and from entanglement in the wheel of Samsara. In positive terms, it is the attainment of unity with the Supreme, the Sat-chit-ananda.

Man is therefore exhorted to utilise his human birth in a proper manner helpful to his higher evolution. For human birth is a very rare good fortune in this universe with countless species of beings. Having got it, if man utilises the brief life-time for the low pleasures of eating and sexual indulgences, which can be had even in animal bodies, and bestows no attention on Dharma and Moksha, he is like one committing suicide. While a man may have the legitimate pleasures and possessions in life, he will be debasing his human heritage if he is making these the be-all and the end-all of his life. His moral and spiritual evolution, the special development possible in human embodiment, will thereby be arrested. His condition may remain a stalemate or undergo degeneration even upto the animal level. But there is no perdition for the Jiva as threatened by Semetic religions. His basic divine nature cannot be obliterated, and he can rise up again, however much he might have degenerated.

It is not by succumbing to the animal instincts, but by subordinating them through sense control that man rises in the scale of evolution. Hence utmost importance is given to self-control. The right course of evolution for him lies through the pursuit of Dharma and Moksha. Dharma includes the discharge of all his religious and secular duties, practice of charity and participation in disinterested and altruistic works, and cultivation of noble traits of character like patriotism and humanitarianism. By such means he has to expand from the self-centredness of the natural man. For, to be self-centred is vice and to live for others is virtue.

By morality alone the Jiva cannot attain the summum bonum of life. While morality is a very necessary attainment for higher evolution, it is Bhakti and Jnana (love of God and spiritual enlightenment) alone that can unite the Jiva, the Spirit in man, with Brahman, the Universal Spirit, of whom the Jiva is a particle like a spark from a fire. Bhakti and Jnana constitute the Sadhana, the means, for union with the Supreme Spirit, the Sat-chit-ananda.

For the successful practice of Sadhana man should have an aversion for the vulgar enjoyments of life and a burning aspiration for the attainment of the Divine. The more powerful these are in him, the more fruitful would be his efforts. He should study the scriptures and gain from them a knowledge of God as experienced and expounded by great sages and incarnations. He should seek a spiritual teacher in whom he has complete faith. Faith in the teacher and in the scriptural teachings are the two most important requirements in a spiritual aspirant. A study of the Upanishads, the Gita and some of the Puranas will give an adequate understanding of the theory about God, the Soul and Nature, as also of what Moksha (liberation) means. But the Vedanta does not stop with a theoretical acceptance of a creed, a dogma, or a set of teachings, nor with the performance of certain ceremonials and adopting certain ways of life. The fundamental verities it teaches, God and the Atman, have to become a matter of experience for the aspirant. So in the religion of the Vedanta there is insistence on Sadhana—in the practice of discrimination, renunciation and meditation as instructed by the teacher. Realisation of the presence of the Divine in oneself and in all beings is the final consummation of all these endeavours. The evolution of the Jiva's potentialities through repeated embodiments is complete when, at the maturity of his Sadhana, he is able to abandon his individual ego through an unconditional surrender to the Supreme Being and thus realise his true self in Him. Then will the 'I' disappear in the 'He'.

III THE PERSONAL-IMPERSONAL ISWARA

In this brief statement of the Vedantic world view, many of its important philosophical and theological tenets have been touched upon briefly. We can recapitulate them and add a few more points wherever necessary by way of elucidation in the following paragraphs:

The first and foremost teaching of Vedantism is the belief in a Godhead, described in the Vedantic terminology as Sat-chit-ananda Parabrahman—the Supreme Being who is Existence-Knowledge-Bliss. In the concept of the Supreme Being there are two aspects—He is on the one hand the Absolute, the unrelated and transcendent, by the side of whom there is no second to limit Him; on the other He is also God, the creator of the world system, who can be worshipped, approached and communed with. In other words, He is transcendent and yet immanent at the same time—the farthest of the far and the nearest of the near. These two contradictory characteristics of Paratva (transcendence) and Saulabhya (easy availability) meet in the Vedantic conception of the Supreme Being. The concept of God or Iswara must necessarily be personal and relational; for His is the Will that expresses as the creation, and He is also the possessor of all auspicious attributes like mercy, justice, love, beauty, etc. Above all, He is responsive to man's prayers and adoration. Man can think of such a Being only as a Person. Love, responsiveness, and similar qualities of the heart and head, we experience only in human beings and not in impersonal forces of Nature like electricity, or heat, or gravitation. So a God possessing the noblest attributes, qualities and virtues that the human mind can conceive of must necessarily be a Person, whatever else He be. We have to go a step further. If He is a Person possessing auspicious characteristics, we must also accept that He can have a form, too. For, we cannot think of a virtuous person without an ideal form also. So in Vedantic theology God is conceived as the Supreme Person with an ideal Form, and those monotheistic critics of Vedanta who shrink from a God with a form would do well to abandon their monotheism for the sake of consistency.

But God conceived in this way will be a finite being, one among the many, a person with hands and feet and character of responsiveness like an exalted man. So the Vedanta says He is also the Transcendent Impersonal and Absolute Being (Nirguna and Nishprapancha). But for us, whose limited intelligence would permit us to think of a person alone as intelligent and possessed of auspicious qualities, it is impossible to understand an impersonal entity to be Chit (consciousness) and Ananda (bliss). Two alternatives are left. We can go with Spinoza and say that God is ever the Absolute only, to whose level one can rise and with whom one can become united, but to whom it is futile to pray; for, He neither hears nor responds as He is not a Person. Or one can side with some of the modern Western philosophers and accept the theory of a limited God. But a God limited ceases to be the Supreme Being just as a God who is only the Infinite and the Absolute ceases to be of any value for man. Truth if it is not a value is a myth, and value if it is not true is an illusion.

So both the above mentioned views of the Supreme Being are unsatisfactory to the religious conscience. Worship of a God who is not also the Absolute is idolatry, and a mere Absolute, who is characterless and irresponsive, is not better than matter. The Vedanta therefore accepts the Supreme Being as both Personal and Impersonal. When the votary in the course of his spiritual development becomes de-personalised on achieving the elimination of his ego-based body-mind, he will be able to understand the true Impersonal. Till then, that is, so long as he is a person, the Impersonal and the Absolute can only mean for him a Personal Being who is much more than what he, a person, has grasped or can grasp of Him. To illustrate, the Impersonal-Personal Divine of the Vedanta is the ocean, and the God of adoration of the devotee is like a big field or backwater into which the water of that ocean has flowed. The many deities that form the object of worship of Vedantism are like these tanks and backwaters in the analogy. They are so many manifestations of the Personal-Impersonal

Sat-chit-ananda in the thought structures of those who adore Him, or are forms adopted by Him for the achievement of cosmic purposes in His world-play. The worship of these forms with an understanding of the infinitude that informs their finitude, may be called the Vedantic Polytheism (Polytheism with a capital P), which is the only form of true worship that the human mind is capable of, so long as man remains a limited person. The other ideas of the Divine which Semitic religions hold—their so-called boasted monotheism—is only a form of disguised idolatry; for when it is said that Jehova is a jealous God, or that there is no God but Allah, it is obvious that the Supreme Being is identified as an exclusive individual and not as an expression of an Infinite Being in terms of the human mind. When the link with the Infinite is forgotten, a Deity, whether it is a monotheistic entity or a polytheistic being, becomes a mere idol. Real worship of the Supreme Being is possible only when the principle of Vedantic Polytheism is understood—that principle being the perception of the infinite Personal-Impersonal Being through a limited and humanised manifestation of Him.

A Vedantic Deity is never aggressive, demanding the overthrow of other deities. But a monotheistic Deity, always a jealous God, cannot tolerate another Deity. As Toynbee has pointed out, the monotheistic Deity of the Semitics is only an apotheosis of the group or tribal consciousness of certain people, a sentiment that held together societies before nationalism took its place. Just as the nationalistic patriotism is eager to absorb all other countries, that form of group consciousness masquerading as monotheism wants to supplant all other religions and establish its Deity in their sanctuaries. Proselytism, for which many religions stand but which has no place in the Vedantic scheme, is the consequence of entertaining a God who is not an expression of the Infinite Being but a personalisation of the group consicousness of a people.

This kind of an analysis of the devotional attitude and the concept of the Deity has become necessary because the modern anthropologists have interpreted the religion of India equating it with the polytheism that they have found in primitive societies, and because many among us, who have studied their views, have come to accept them without an understanding of the profound philosophic basis of Vedantic Polytheism.

The principle enunciated above in regard to Deities is applicable also to worship of God in holy images, which critics, who are practising real idolatry, have stigmatised as idolatry. The Vedantin's God is not an individual as of the Semite's. He is the Universal Spirit who has manifested as All-Nature. He is one with all, and if a person with faith wants to see Him anywhere, He is present there. Like water running all through the ground, He is everywhere; and, if the well of faith is dug, He becomes available for worship. A holy image is thus a point at which His real presence is available for imperfect man to apprehend and commune with. It is not a mere means for practising concentration as some apologists say. It is much more. It is a point of real communion with the Divine when the eye of faith reveals Him as accepting the worship and offering made by the devotee. It is in this spirit that all the great sages and saviours of India, down to Bhagavan Sri Ramakrishna, have seen and adored the Holy Images. Its practice is one of the most excellent and necessary aids for the vast majority of men to gradually rise in the spiritual scale. The Divine presence is made concrete, and prayers and adoration made meaningful to those men who cannot dive into the depths of consicousness by meditation and introspection and commune with the subtle Spirit as the Inner Pervader within. It is therefore a necessary step in practising religion as an experience instead of reducing it to an expression of conformity with a dogmatic creed or adherence to some formal code of conduct and rituals.

IV THE JIVA OR THE INDIVIDUAL SPIRIT

Acceptance of a Jiva, the individual soul, is another important tenet of Vedantic religion. Without it, the ideas of conservation of moral and spiritual values, of Karma and re-birth, and of liberation from Samsara become meaningless. An embodied living Spirit is called a Jiva. The Jiva is the embodied Atman in evolution. He is by nature perfect, being a spark from the fire that is the Divine. But, from a beginningless past he has been under the bondage of Karma and therefore embodied in a material medium for reaping the fruits of Karma. Through repeated births, he evolves better bodies reflecting the glory of the Spirit. This is a doctrine that has already been explained in the theory of Samsara. In Jivahood the Atman, indentified himself with its body, and does not experience his distinctiveness as the Atman except in theory when instructed by the scripture and the teacher. But none the less the Atman does not lose his divine nature and potentiality in spite of identification with the body, just as flint kept in water does not lose its fire-producing efficiency. Evolution is the repeated embodiment of the Jiva in better and better body-minds that provide a field for manifesting his inherent divinity. The process of evolution goes on until the Jiva discovers his spiritual identity as the unaffected and unchangeable Atman, which is a part and parcel of the Supreme Divinity. This attainment is Moksha.

A Jiva or the Atman embodied is spoken of as having five vestments, which form three bodies. The five vestments are Annamaya-kosa, the physical sheath; the Pranamaya-kosa, the vitalistic sheath; Manomaya-kosa, the mental sheath; Vijnanamaya-kosa, the sheath of self-consciousness and rationality; and Anandamaya-kosa, the sheath of bliss. At the core enshrouded by these is the Divine Spark, the Atman, whose light of intelligence and self-consciousness percolates through these sheaths and makes the inert sheaths luminous with consciousness, as a central flame illumines several shades covering it. The five sheaths form the three bodies of the Jiva. The outermost sheath, the Annamaya-kosa forms the physical body which perishes at death, with the prospect of a new such body being formed for the Jiva when re-born according to his Karma. Even when the Annamaya-kosa perishes, the other sheaths survive as the subtle body or Linga Sarira, which transmigrates as the vehicle of the Atman till the attainment of Moksha or release from Samsara. The subtle body carries with it all the impressions and efficiencies derived from previous births as the Karma-potential of the Jiva. At death, the Jiva, clothed in the subtle body may remain in a state of slumber, in which consciousness is in abeyance, until he gets a new body. Or he may go along the Path of Smoke or the Path of Light to Pitri Loka or Deva Loka, where he will get celestial bodies to enjoy the fruits of his exceedingly good Karmas. When such Karmas are exhausted, he loses his celestial body, and has to come to earth again for acquiring new Karma or gaining spiritual perfection. The process of birth, death and moving from sphere to sphere goes on till the Jiva attains the knowledge of his nature as Sat-chit-ananda, when his link with the body called Hridayagranthi is cut asunder, and he attains Moksha or liberation.

What is the ontological status of the Jiva and how does he stand in relation with God, is a problem that is taken up in the Vedanta metaphysics for discussion. The Vedanta does not accept the Christian and Muslim theory that the Jiva is created or brought into existence from nothing by the Creator at the time of the birth of the body. The Advaitins or the monists maintain that ultimately the Jiva is one with Brahman, though in bondage he may appear to be different. This apparent difference is illustrated with the example of a reflection of the sun in water. In the medium of many water receptacles, the sun shines as so many images of himself, and when the water receptacles are eliminated, only the one universal sun remains. All the reflections relapse into the sun. Similarly, the Jiva has no separate existence from Iswara. The body-mind evolved by Maya is the reflector in which the Sat-chit-ananda casts His reflection, and that reflection is the Jiva. So long as the reflection is identified with the reflecting medium, all the movements and distortions of that medium become the characteristics of the sun's image in it also, though these do not affect the matrix, the universal sun. When the medium is eliminated by enlightenment, the Jiva as reflection relapses into its matrix, the Sat-chit-ananda Parabrahman.

Another school of Vedanta would consider the Jiva as the Pure Consciousness circumscribed by the body-mind, like the sky limited by a pot. Just as the pot-sky becomes one with the universal sky when the pot is destroyed, the Jiva becomes one with the Supreme Being, when he is liberated from the limitation imposed by the body-mind. In both these views of Advaita, the Jiva has no ultimacy. In liberation it is identical with Brahman, and from an ontological point of view the difference from Brahman is only apparent.

In schools of Vedanta that are not non-dualistic, the Jiva is ultimate. In liberation he is freed from Samsara and the subtle body which is the cause of Samsara. The Jiva then gets a celestial body of Suddha-sattva, and he becomes the servant of God in the transcendental realm (Vaikuntha). Both in bondage and liberation, the Jiva is a distinct entity, a speak of self-conscious existence having an identity of his own. In bondage his knowledge is contracted, and in liberation it expands, and becomes coterminous with that of the Lord, though his entity still remains separate. Some schools speak of the Jiva and Nature as existences eternally separate but absolutely dependent on Iswara. Others like the school of Visishtadvaita forge a greater unity between Iswara and the Jiva-Jagat (soul and the world) by positing an organismic relation between them. An organism, say a human body, contains millions of cells, each cell being an individual in itself forming an inseparable part of the whole, the body. They participate in the life of the whole, and exist for subserving the purpose of the whole they embody. Such is the relation of the Jivas in regard to Iswara. Though individually they are separate and would remain so always, they form a unity inseparable from the Whole, sharing the life of the Whole, subserving the purpose of the Master-Being in the Whole, namely Iswara. That totality forming what may be called the Cosmic All-inclusive Organism or Whole is Brahman, the Infinite and the Absolute Being, in the system of qualified non-dualism. The transcendent Iswara is the inner soul of the Whole as also of every part of It. He is thus the Para (different, trancendent and unaffected) on the one hand, and on the other, also the Sulabha, one near and dear and easily available for purposes of worship and adoration, being the inner pervader of all. Thus the Whole, with the Jivas and Nature forming the body and Iswara the soul, is called Brahman in this system.

V PRAKRITI OR NATURE

The third important category is Prakriti or Nature, of which matter is an evolute. In addition to the theory of God and Jiva, theological speculation requires a material stuff, of which the universe is formed. Semitic religions speak of God creating out of nothing the universe of matter and souls at the beginning of time. But as it has been already pointed out in explaining the theory of Samsara, the Vedanta does not accept such a view of creation. Creation does not mean a first beginning, but beginning of a cycle of manifestation. The Sanskrit word for creation is Srishti, which means projecting something from the subtle into a gross condition, and not bringing a totally non-existent thing into existence. The universe in its causal condition is called Prakriti. Prakriti is not an independent substance, but an energy that forms a part and parcel of the Supreme Being, Iswara. It is described as a Power or Sakti of the Lord. The Lord and His Sakti are one, just as fire and its heat and luminosity and are. Though one with fire, they are distinguishable from it. The heat and the luminosity may be converted into various forms of effects. Though all these effects are in one sense based on fire, they do not affect the fire. Similar is the relation between Iswara and His Sakti, or His power of manifestation into this most wonderful universe. Iswara, through Prakriti, His Sakti, is thus both the material and the efficient cause of the universe. Though there is a multiplicity in the created world, they are all based on, and resolvable into, the unitary principle, Brahman.

Sattva, Rajas and Tamas are the threefold expression of Prakriti. They are called Gunas, which are both substance and attributes. They stand for equilibrium, movement and inertia, or, for peace, passion, and sleep and other states and qualities allied to them. When the Gunas are in equilibrium, Prakriti is in a state of equifoise, and all creative activity is at a stand-still. This is the state of Pralaya. When at the will of the Lord the Gunas begin to stir, Prakriti is agitated and starts on that course of evolution which brings into being the twenty-four categories ending with gross matter. Out of these, all the worlds are formed, and the Jivas get their embodiments according to their Karma in bodies constituted of these categories. Brahma is the intermediary principle, through whom this world governance is accomplished by the Supreme Being. His one daytime, which represents four hundred and thirty two million human years, is one Kalpa or period of manifestation of the universe, after which it relapses into the state of abeyance called Pralaya (Brahma's night) lasting for an equally long period. Thus Prakriti, which is a Sakti of the Lord, follows these laws of manifestation and withdrawal for eternity providing Jivas with the field to work out their Karma, to evolve through repeated embodiments, and finally to attain release when enlightenment dawns on them.

V SALVATION OPEN TO ALL

Subject to the acceptance of this world view which is far more credible to the reason of man than any offered by Non-Vedantic religions, a spiritual aspirant is free to choose and follow any form of the Deity, or Incarnation, or World-teacher. Any religious symbol or personality or Deity accepted as an expression of the Supreme Being with absolute faith will take an aspirant to the realisation of his nature as Spirit and to the attainment of salvation in Brahman. Salvation is the sure and certain goal of every embodied being, who attains to that degree of purity of mind required for the practice of Bhakti and Jnana. There is no threat of damnation for not accepting any creed or personality or Deity. Innumerable are the pathways (Sampradayas) that the Supreme Being has revealed for the aspiring souls. Any path is good enough for salvation, provided it is accepted in absolute faith, and provided its teachings tend towards the generation of renunciation, devotion and surrender.

There are many Sampradayas or theological traditions that follow cults based on the Vedantic world view. Such are the cults of Vishnu, Siva and the Mother Goddess, each of which has several sub-cults with their variations of the cult deity, form of worship and meditation. There is no objection to add to these any other cult like those of Christ or of the Buddha. In modern times the cult of Ramakrishna is gaining wide acceptance among those who follow the Vedantic world view. Whatever the cult followed, the Vedanta has evolved a three-pronged Sadhana for spiritual aspirants, these being known as Karma Yoga, Bhakti Yoga and Jnana Yoga. A serious spiritual aspirant must undergo spiritual practices based on any one or more of the Yogas or all of them combined. The Vedantic scriptures exhort man again and again that unless he practises some Sadhana for spiritual realisation, his precious human life is a wasted opportunity that is difficult to get again. Thus, according to the Vedanta, religion is an absolute necessity for man, if he is to live a really human life.

Madras SWAMI TAPASYANANDA
April, 1981.

A Primer of Hinduism

CHAPTER I

OUR GUIDES

I

DAUGHTER—Father, are you free now?

FATHER—Yes, my child. What do you want?

D.—Father, you promised that if I should pass the Gītā examination held by the Rajahmundry Hindu Samaj, you would teach me the essentials of Hinduism. Now that I have passed it and also got a prize, you should redeem your promise.

F.—You have passed only the lower examination. Attempt the higher when you go to the sixth form next year and pass it. Then I will teach you. But when once you know your Gītā thoroughly, you don't require any further teaching. All the essentials of Hinduism are there.

D.—But it is so confusing to me, father. In some places it teaches Karma-Yoga and in others Karma-Sannyāsa. I am not able to make it out.

F.—All the same you have passed your examination!

D.—They asked us very simple questions and I was able to answer them fairly well from what you were telling us in the prayer classes in the morning. But the higher examination will be difficult. I am told it requires a general knowledge of Hinduism. So if you teach me the essentials of our religion, I will sit for the higher examination next year.

F.—Well, I have no objection my child, to teach you what I know, if you are so anxious to learn. But how shall we proceed? If I proceed to give you a long account of the essentials of Hinduism, I am sure you will soon be tired. Suppose you put me some questions every day and I try to answer them, would that method suit you?

D.—I don't know what questions to put. But I have no objection to this method, if after one or two questions, you suggest to me further questions by means of your answers.

F.—I will try.

II

D.—First of all, who is the founder of Hinduism? We read that Buddhism was founded by Buddha. Christianity by Christ, and Mohammedanism by Mohammed. But who founded Hinduism?

F.—It is one of the distinctive features of Hinduism that it has no founder. It does not depend for its authority on the life-history of any man.

D.—What is its authority then?

F.—Its authority is Eternal Truth itself to which every man's spiritual experience can bear witness.

D.—I have no spiritual experience of any kind. How am I to know the Eternal Truth?

F.—As the spiritual experience of almost all men is imperfect, Truth revealed itself in this land through the minds of great Ṛṣis. And this revelation is embodied in the Śruti.

D.—What is Śruti?

F.—'Śruti' literally means what is heard. Great Ṛṣis who had perfected themselves by long *tapas* are said to have heard in their hearts eternal truths and to have left a record of them in our sacred books.

D.—What are these sacred books?

F.—They are called the Vedas—the Ṛg-veda, the Sāma-veda, the Yajur-veda and Atharvaṇa-veda.

D.—Are the Vedas then the authorities for Hinduism?

F.—Yes. The Vedas claim to teach a man the highest truths that he can know and to lead him to his highest good. They are therefore supremely authoritative. And as Truth is eternal, the Vedas which have revealed it to the Hindus are also considered by them to be eternal.

D.—What do the Vedas consist of?

F.—Each Veda consists of four parts—(1) the Mantras or hymns; (2) the Brāhmaṇas or explanatory treatises on mantras and rituals; (3) the Āraṇyakas or meditations in the forest and (4) the Upaniṣads or mystic treatises revealing the most profound spiritual truths and suggesting the ways of realizing them.

D.—Are all these parts equally important? Is every word of the Veda sacred?

F.—Will you tell me whether each rose plant is equally alive from the root to the flower? Without the root, the stem, the leaves and even the thorns how can we have the flower? The Upaniṣad is the rose and it grows naturally out of the Vedic hymns and sacrifices. It is the most important part of the Veda.

D.—So we have four Upaniṣads for the four Vedas?

F.—No. Each Veda contains many Upaniṣads.

D.—How many Upaniṣads have we then on the whole?

F.—The Upaniṣads are many in number. But twelve of them are considered the most important.

D.—What are they?

F.—They are,—Īśa, Kena, Kaṭha, Praśna, Muṇḍaka, Māṇḍūkya, Aitareya, Taittirīya Chāndogya, Bṛhadāraṇyaka, Kauṣītakī and Śvetāśvatara.

D.—Why are these considered the important?

F.—Because they contain the highest truths known to Hinduism.

D.—Are these the only authorities for Hinduism?

F.—The Śruti is, of course, the primary authority. But we have a number of secondary authorities based on the Śruti. Of these first comes the Smṛti.

D.—What does the Smṛti consist of?

F.—The Smṛti consists of admittedly human compositions, the object of which is to regulate personal and social life and to bring into existence institutions embodying the principles of the Śruti. Therefore the laws for regulating Hindu society from time to time are codified in the Smṛti.

D.—Do the laws change from time to time?

F.—Yes. The Ṛṣis who guide Hindu society from age to age make the necessary alterations in the laws according to the needs of the time.

D.—So Hinduism allows the introduction of new laws?

F.—Most certainly it does. It allows not only the introduction of new laws but also the production of new scriptures. Else it would be a dead religion.

D.—Who are the most important law-givers of the past?

F.—The Most important Hindu law-givers are Manu, Yājñavalkya and Parāśara.

D.—What are the subjects they deal with in their codes?

F.—They deal with Dharma or the duty of the various classes of citizens. Hence their law books are known as Dharma-Śāstras. They give detailed instructions regarding the duties of a man according to his class and station in life. They also describe the duties of kings, the administration of civil and criminal law, the sanitary measures adopted in ancient times and the penances prescribed for various sins.

3

D.—Is our society strictly bound to follow these instructions now?

F.—I have already said that laws change from time to time. Social and political institutions grow, men's ideas change, and new factors are introduced into national life. Then some of the old laws become obsolete and new conventions arise, which, in course of time under the lead of great Ṛṣis, come to be established as laws. Hindu society has ever been a living organism and its codes of laws always flexible.

D.—Is it a living organism now?

F.—It is. It has survived many foreign invasions. It has seen many empires rise and fall. It is as strong today as when Alexander the Great invaded India.

D.—But are its codes now flexible?

F.—Hindu society is slowly adjusting itself to the needs of the present time. Only these adjustments are not properly codified and made authoritative. The real test of life in any organism lies in the response it gives to the environment. If our society at any time fails to respond to the needs of the hour, if it fails to follow the lead of its living sages, and if it has not the imagination and the courage to march on and give a new embodiment to the eternal principles of unity, brotherhood and love declared by the Śruti, it will surely perish, and Hindus will go the way of the ancient Greeks and Romans.

D.—So the laws of the Smṛti are entirely subordinate to the eternal principles of the Śruti?

F.—Yes. The relation of the Smṛti to the Śruti is similar to that of the body to the soul. The body grows. It decays and dies. It is subject to the time-process, while the soul is not. The latter is beyond time.

D.—What are the other secondary authorities besides the Smṛti?

F.—Next to the Smṛtis or the codes of law, we have the Itihāsas, the Purāṇas, the Āgamas and the Darśanas. Let me tell you, in passing, that sometimes the word Smṛti is used in a wider sense, so as to include all these secondary scriptures.

D.—Are these also subject to change?

F.—Yes. If the Śruti is the soul and the Smṛti is the body, these are only organs and limbs.

D.—What are Itihāsas? And what is their object?

F.—The Itihāsas are the two well-known epics—the Rāmāyaṇa and Mahābhārata. Their object is to drive home to the popular mind, by means of history and legend, the principles of the Veda and the laws of Smṛti. The great types of character that we find in these books have firmly established the Hindu Dharma in the mind of our nation.

D.—So they form a sort of popular Veda?

F.—Exactly. The Śruti, on account of the elaborate rituals and the long courses of discipline it prescribes, could only be for the few. But the Epics and the Purāṇas, which are only popular renderings of the Vedic truths, are for all. Almost all Hindus get their earliest religious notions from the stories in the popular Veda. Have you not read these stories?

D.—Yes, father, I have. So Vālmīki and Vyāsa, the

authors of the two epics, have to be looked upon as the Ṛṣis who have popularized the teachings of the Veda.

F.—Yes. Moreover they are great nation-builders. Hindu society is still following the lines chalked out by them. The characters they have created in the epics are more real to us than those in actual life. Every Hindu child knows that Rāma is an ideal king, that Sītā is an ideal wife according to Hindu conceptions, and that Lakṣmaṇa and Hanumān represent the Hindu ideals of loyalty, devotion, and discipline.

D.—And what about the characters in the Mahābhārata?

F.—The Mahābhārata is primarily an encyclopaedia of Hindu Dharma. It consists of long stories, episodes, dialogues, discourses and sermons. However, the divine figure of Śri Kṛṣṇa dominates the whole. He holds all the strings of action. He is represented both as a great teacher and a man of action. Next to him come the five Pāṇḍavas, headed by Yudhiṣṭhira who is the very embodiment of Hindu Dharma in peace and war. Another great character who is an authority on Hindu Dharma is the old warrior Bhīṣma. His lengthy discourses in Śāntiparva are justly famous.

D.—But is not the Bhagavad Gītā the most important discourse on Hindu Dharma in this epic?

F.—Undoubtedly it is.

D.—What is its importance due to?

F.—Its importance is due both to its context and its contents. Firstly, you know it occurs just before the momentous battle between the Pāṇḍavas and Kauravas on the field of Kurukṣetra. The discourse between Kṛṣṇa and Arjuna is placed at the very focus of the great epic, the point towards which the actions of all the characters tend and from which their subsequent fates diverge. At the critical moment, when Arjuna saw his dear kinsmen ranged against him in the battle, he grew faint of heart and was tempted to relinquish his duty as a soldier. If he had done so, there would have been an end of the war, and the evil embodied in Duryodhana and his allies would have triumphed. But this calamity was averted by Kṛṣṇa. He came to the rescue of Arjuna, discussed with him the moral and the metaphysical implications of all human duties, removed his doubts and made him perform the task before him in a dispassionate and fearless manner. Secondly, the Gītā gives in a nutshell all the philosophical and the ethical teachings of the Upaniṣads. There is a well-known verse which compares the Upaniṣads to cows, the Gītā to milk, Kṛṣṇa to a cowherd and Arjuna to a calf. Moreover the Gītā shows a profound knowledge of the human heart—its hopes and needs, its doubts and difficulties and its trials and temptations. Also, it aims at producing a type of character which is the loftiest that the Hindu imagination has ever conceived. For, the ideal Yogin of the Bhagavad-Gītā is, like the Avatār himself, both a man of contemplation and a man of action—a practical mystic whose head is in solitude and whose hands are in society.

D.—Is the teaching of the Gītā as authoritative as that of the Śruti?

F.—Yes. The Gītā, being the essence of the Upaniṣads, is considered as authoritative as the Śruti. It is one of the three prasthānas or authoritative scriptures.

D.—What are the other two prasthānas?

F.—The other two are the Upaniṣads and the Brahma-sūtras or Vedānta-sūtras.

D.—What are the Brahma-sūtras?

F.—The Brahma-sūtras are a number of aphorisms which systematize the whole teaching of the Upaniṣads.

D.—Who is their author?

F.—Bādarāyaṇa is the author of the Brahma-sūtras.

D.—Why are the Brahma-sūtras so called?

F.—They are called Brahma-sūtras, because they expound the nature of Brahman or the Absolute and its relation to man and the world.

D.—Why are they also called the Vedānta-sūtras?

F.—Vedānta means the end of the Veda. The Upaniṣads, being the final portions of the Veda, are called Vedānta. And because the sūtras string together the flowers of the Vedānta passages they are called Vedānta-sūtras.

D.—If the sūtras are brief aphorisms, how can we understand from them the whole teaching of the Vedānta?

F.—There are elaborate commentaries on the sūtras written by eminent philosophers and theologians like Śaṁkara, Rāmānuja and Madhva. It is these that have given rise to the various schools of the Vedānta-darśana.

D.—But you mentioned Purāṇas and Āgamas before Darśanas. I should like to know something about them. What are Purāṇas?

F.—Purāṇas are religious stories which illustrate the truths of the Śruti by means of stories of kings, adventures of gods and legends of saints. They were the means employed by Hindu teachers of a later age for purposes of mass education. And you know that many beautiful stories such as those of Prahlāda and Dhruva come to us from the Purāṇas.

D.—Are not the accounts given in the Purāṇas historically true?

F.—Some of them may have a historical basis. But most of them are obviously imaginative. We may call them historical parables in which facts and fiction are combined as in historical dramas or historical novels. The Hindu scriptures deal with ideal truth, and not with historical truth. Their validity does not depend on any historical fact. This is very well illustrated in the accounts we have in the Purāṇas of the various Avatārs of Viṣṇu. For these are intended to give only an imaginative representation of the help rendered by God to man at different stages of his evolution.

D.—What is an Avatār?

F.—An Avatār is an incarnation of God. When God comes down and lives in the flesh for any special purpose we call Him an Avatār.

D.—What is the special purpose of an Avatār?

F.—Don't you remember the well-known verses in the Gītā which explain the purpose of an Avatār?

"Whenever there is decay of Dharma, O Arjuna, and an outbreak of adharma I embody myself. For the protection of the good, for the destruction of the wicked, and for the establishment of Dharma I am born from age to age."

D.—How many Avatārs are there?

F.—The Bhāgavata Purāṇa says:—

"The Avatārs of Viṣṇu are innumerable like the streams flowing from an inexhaustible lake."

But in popular Hinduism ten Avatārs are recognized.

D.—What are they?

F.—They are: (1) Matsya (the Fish), (2) Kūrma (The Tortoise), (3) Varāha (the Boar), (4) Narasimha (The Man-lion), (5) Vāmana (The Dwarf), (6) Paraśurāma, (7) Rāma, (8) Kṛṣṇa, (9) Buddha and (10) Kalki. It will be seen that some of these are purely mythological, some legendary, some historical, and the last is purely prophetic.

D.—Is Buddha also an Avatār?

F.—Yes. He is among the great teachers of mankind. In spite of some doctrinal differences between Hinduism and Buddhism, the Hindus look upon Buddha as one of themselves and recognize the value of the service he has rendered to true religion. Jayadeva, for instance, in his famous lyric poem, Gītā Govindam, praises Viṣṇu as the great God who, under the guise of Buddha, taught us kindness to all living beings and prohibited animal sacrifices.

D.—So is Buddhism a part of Hinduism like Vaiṣṇavism or Śaivism?

F.—Well, Buddhism is an off-shoot of Hinduism. Many of

its doctrines and ideals are the same as those of Hinduism. Buddha himself lived and died a Hindu. He looked upon himself more as a reformer than as an innovator. And yet Buddhism is not considered strictly orthodox by us now like Vaiṣṇavism or Śaivism, because Buddhists do not recognize the authority of the Veda. However, this does not prevent us from looking upon Buddha as an Avatār.

D.—Are the Avatārs confined to India?

F.—Certainly not. In the verse that I have quoted from the Gītā describing the purpose of an Avatār, no geographical or chronological limitations are indicated. There is no mention of any particular country or age.

D.—So there may be Avatārs in the future also?

F.—Yes. For God has not ceased to exist. Nor has He ceased to care for His creatures. He is not so partial as to reveal Himself only to a particular nation or in a particular country or age. He reveals Himself whenever there is need of His grace and loving kindness. Our Purāṇas say so explicitly. As a matter of fact, one of the Purāṇas foretells a tenth Avatār. Hinduism makes for a progressive realization of Truth. It undoubtedly contemplates the advent of new Avatārs, as it does the promulgation of new laws and the proclamation of new gospels. Hinduism does not bury its head in the past; nor does it rebelliously secede from the past. So it is not impossible, my child, that even now, while we are speaking here, the sacred feet of a new Avatār may be marching across the plains of Hindusthan, interpreting our ancient Dharma in terms of modern life, and taking up the message of love and ahimsā from where Buddha left it.

D.—And, like new Avatārs, there may be also new Purāṇas in future?

F.—Certainly, as the genius of our race is still alive.

D.—How many Purānas have we already?

F.—There are eighteen chief Purāṇas of which the most popular are the Viṣṇu Purāṇa and the Bhāgavata Purāṇa. In fact, the latter is so important in its influence on the religious imagination of India that it is placed on the same level as the Rāmāyana and the Mahābhārata.

III

D.—Then what are Āgamas?

F.—The word Āgama generally means a scripture. But, in its narrow sense, it is used to denote a class of sectarian scriptures dealing with the worship of a particular aspect of God and prescribing detailed courses of discipline for the worshipper. As their aim is thus intensely practical they are known as sādhanaśāstra.

D.—How many Āgamas are there?

F.—The Āgamas, like the Upaniṣads, are many in number. But they can be divided into three main groups, according as the deity that forms the object of worship is Viṣṇu, Śiva or Śakti. These three groups have given rise to the three main branches of Hinduism, namely, Vaiṣṇavism, Śaivism and Śāktism. The Vaiṣṇava-āgamas, or Pāncarātra-āgamas, glorify the Supreme under one of the names and forms of Viṣṇu. The Śaiva-āgamas glorify the Supreme under one of the names and forms of Śiva, and have given rise to an important school of philosophy, known as Śaiva Siddhānta. The Śākta-āgamas or Tantras glorify the Supreme as the mother of the universe under one of the names and forms of Devi.

D.—What does each Āgama consist of?

F.—Each Āgama consists of four sections: (1) philosophy, (2) mental discipline, (3) rules for constructing temples and images and (4) religious practices. Of course, these are all more or less technical matters. But the importance of the Āgamas lies in the wonderful mass of devotional poetry that has sprung up around them in the vernaculars of India. This shows that the Āgamas have succeeded in bringing religion home to the hearts of common people.

D.—Are all these Āgamas based on the Śruti?

F.—Yes. Else they would not be authoritative. Some of them may have originated independently of the Veda. But, when the communities that produced them entered the Hindu fold they came under the influence of the Veda, were thoroughly imbued with its spirit and accepted its authority. A great Vaiṣṇava teacher Yāmunācārya discusses the relation of Vaiṣṇava-āgamas to the Vedas and establishes that the former are Vedic in spirit and hence authoritative. The Śaivite commentator Śrīkaṇṭa says, "We see no difference between the Veda and the Śaiva Āgama." Similarly, a great Śaivite writer called Meykaṇḍar says of the scriptures of his sect, "The Āgamas are special and revealed for the benefit of the blessed, and they contain the essential truths of the Veda and Vedānta." So there is no doubt that in spite of their immense diversity in forms and methods of worship, the Āgamas are thoroughly Vedic in spirit and character.

D.—You say that the communities that produced some of the Āgamas entered the Hindu fold at one time. Does Hinduism make converts?

F.—Yes. Hinduism, no doubt, does not carry on any aggressive propaganda or make forcible conversions or abuse other religions. But in the course of its history it has peacefully absorbed many communities and changed the character of their religion, while allowing them to retain their customs and manners, and their rites and ceremonies.

D.—Now, lastly, we come to the Darśanas. What are Darśanas?

F.—Darśanas are schools of philosophy based again on the Śruti. Each school tries to correlate, systematize and develop the teachings of the various parts of the Veda. Here the appeal is to the logical understanding, while in the Purāṇas, it is to the imagination, and in the Āgamas it is to the heart.

D.—How many Darśanas are there?

F.—We have six Darśanas.

D.—What are they?

F.—They are Nyāya, Vaiśeṣika, Sāṁkhya, Yoga, Mīmāṁsā and Vedānta. But they are divided into three groups on account of their resemblances in doctrine:—(1) Nyāya-Vaiśeṣika (2) Sāṁkhya-Yoga and (3) Mīmāṁsā-Vedānta.

D.—Are the names of the founders of these schools known?

F.—Yes. Nyāya was founded by Gautama, Vaiśeṣika by

Kaṇāda, Sāṁkhya by Kapila, Yoga by Patañjali, Mīmāmsā by Jaimini and Vedānta by Bādarāyaṇa.

D.—What does each Darśana consist of?

F.—It consists of a number of sūtras or aphorisms by the founder in which he gives out his theory. To these is attached an authoritative commentary of a later age. And then there are glosses, and commentaries on the original commentary.

D.—Are these six Darśanas equally authoritative?

F.—Each Darśana has had its day. It is the Vedānta alone that now holds the field as the most satisfactory system of philosophy that could be evolved out of the Upaniṣads.

D.—Why is it considered more satisfactory than the others?

F.—It is considered more satisfactory than the others for three reasons:—firstly, because it duly subordinates individual reason to the revelation of the Veda; secondly, because it has a right conception of the relative importance of the various parts of the Veda; and, thirdly, because it is able to give the most satisfactory answers to all the difficult questions that vex the hearts of religious men.

D.—Is individual reason always to be subordinated to the revelation of the Veda?

F.—Yes. For if every individual were to follow his own reason, there would be chaos and no organized religion. Moreover the mechanism of human knowledge, consisting of perception and inference, is of use to us only in understanding this world of time and space. But to understand the nature of God, who is above these, we have to supplement the testimony of the senses and reason by something else. And this is Śabda or the testimony of the Veda. Thus, in matters of religion, we have three main pramāṇas or testimonies, namely, perception, inference and scripture. The Veda, as pramāṇa, is impersonal, independent and eternal. Therefore mere individual reason has to be subordinated to it. Perception and inference, which are our primary instruments in matter of worldly knowledge, are only secondary here. Their function is only to elucidate the revelation of the Veda.

D.—Is the Veda then an arbitrary authority overriding our own individual experience?

F.—No. On the other hand, in the noble words of Śaṁkara, the knowledge of Brahman taught by the Veda reaches its consummation only in the individual spiritual experience. And our experience is valid only in so far as it conforms to the standard of the Veda. The ultimate ground of Hindu religious belief is not merely the arbitrary authority of a religious tradition or a piece of historical evidence or an individual utterance, but facts of experience which could be ascertained by any man, who is prepared to go through the necessary discipline.

D.—Do not the other five schools of philosophy employ the three pramāṇas of perception, inference and scripture?

F.—Yes, they do. But, though in theory they accept the Veda as the supreme authority, many of their doctrines are in flat contradiction to its teaching. The Mīmāṁsā school, no doubt, goes farthest in making the testimony of scriptures supreme. But it does not have a correct idea of the relative importance of the various parts of the Veda. Hence it has been superseded by the Vedānta.

D.—What are the various parts of the Veda, and what their relative importance?

F.—We have already seen that the Veda consists of the Mantras, the Brāhmaṇas, Araṇyakas and the Upaniṣads. But there is another kind of division according to the subject-matter, namely, (1) Karma-kāṇḍa (2) Upāsana-kāṇḍa and (3) Jñāna-kāṇḍa. The first deals with rituals, the second with worship, and the third with the highest knowledge. According to the Mīmāṁsā school of philosophers the Veda is all ritual, and the other two parts are to be taken as only accessories to it. This view is rejected by the Vedānta school, which rightly believes that Jñāna-kāṇḍa is the most important and the other two are accessories to it. On account of its right conception of the relative importance of the Pramāṇas and the teaching of the Veda, the Vedānta-Darśana has superseded all the other Darśanas and still holds the field.

D.—Father, are all these scriptures which you have described the sources of Hinduism?

F.—Yes. The Veda is the main source. It is the fountain-head of all Indian culture. Its rituals and sacrifices lead to Karma-mīmāṁsā. Its upāsanas lead to the bhakti-doctrine. Its philosophical speculations lead to Vedānta. Its metaphysical disquisitions lead to the logic of Nyāya. Its accounts of creation lead to Sāṁkhya. Its descriptions of religious ecstasy lead to Yoga. Its conception of the cosmic law of Ṛta leads to that of the moral law of Karma. And its kings and ṛṣis are the starting-points of our Itihāsas and Purāṇas. We may even say that its occasional protests against sacrifices lead to Buddhism and Jainism. Thus all our secondary scriptures, namely, the Smṛtis, the Itihāsas, the Purāṇas, the Āgamas and the Darśanas only develop one or the other of the numerous aspects of the Veda.

D.—Father, is the order in which you have mentioned these secondary scriptures the historical order?

F.—Well, it is more or less historical, though there is considerable overlapping.

D.—But I should like to know why, if the Veda is our primary scripture, we should not go direct to it without caring for any of these secondary scriptures.

F.—The Veda is like a mine of gold, and the later scriptures are like the gold coins of the various ages. When you want to procure things which would make you comfortable, you should have ready money and not a piece of rock with veins of gold in it, straight from the mine. Of course, every gold coin which is current in the country is ultimately derived from the mine. But it has undergone various processes that make it useful to us at once. The ore has been smelted, the dross has been removed, the true metal has been refined, put into moulds and stamped. Similarly, the golden truths of the Veda have been refined by the wisdom of the ages and presented to us in a useful form in our later scriptures. That is why I recommended to you the Gītā, rather than the Upaniṣads.

D.—Father, when we have so many codes of laws, so many sectarian scriptures and so many schools of philosophy, how can we arrive at a definite homogeneous religion?

F.—My child, India is a land of religious experiment, and Hinduism is not a simple homogeneous religion. Hinduism is rather a name given to a League of Religions. In its comprehensive and tolerant fold we find all types of religions from the highest to the lowest. For it does not force all minds into one groove. It frankly recognizes the various grades of culture that obtain in a community.

D.—But have all these religions a common aim?

F.—Yes. They have a common aim, just as they have a common source. Their aim is to make man a perfect spirit like God. With this end in view they try to create political and social institutions which will enable every man to realize the God in him. Also, they rouse his imagination, they quicken his intellect, they form his character and undertake to guide him along the path of ascent. Those who accept the Hindu scriptures and undergo the disciplines they prescribe are bound to become perfect, free and God-like spirits in the end. This is what we call Mokṣa.

D.—But is Hinduism the only way to the goal? Are all other religions false?

F.—We Hindus consider it a sin to say that any religion is false. The Avatār of the Gītā says, "Howsoever men approach me, even so do I accept them; for, on all sides, whatever path they may choose leads to me, O Arjuna." Therefore Hinduism is the most tolerant as well as the most comprehensive of religions. It lays no claim to any monopoly of wisdom. Its authority is more a principle of continuity than a principle of exclusion. It abhors violent propaganda and forcible conversions. While it takes care to explain its position and absorbs willing followers, it never denounces other religions as false or evil. One of our minor Upaniṣads says, "Cows have many colours, but the milk of all of them is white. Look upon teachers as cows, and knowledge as milk." Therefore with us toleration is not simply a stroke of policy, but an article of faith. We look upon the whole world as a joint family. We welcome with open arms Muslims, Christians, Jews and Parsees as our brethren. We study their scriptures as reverently as our own, and bow before their prophets. And, as for Buddhists and Jains, they are flesh of our flesh and bone of our bone.

CHAPTER II

THE FIRST ASCENT

I

D.—Father, shall we resume our discussion of Hinduism to-day?

F.—Yes, my child. First of all, let me see what you learnt last time.

D.—Last time you gave me a clear idea of all the authorities of Hinduism. You taught me that the Śruti is the primary authority and that the Smṛti, the Itihāsa, the Purāṇa, the Āgama and the Darśana are secondary authorities. The aim of the latter is only to develop, illustrate and embody the principles of the Veda. The primary authority is for all time, but the secondary authorities vary from age to age. You further taught me that the aim of all Hindu scriptures is to make man a perfect spirit like God and to bring into existence institutions which will help him to reach his goal. I take it, therefore, that according to Hinduism man's life on earth is to be considered a journey towards divine perfection.

F.—I think all the great religions of the world agree in that. The path is the same, though it has different names. And we should always bear in mind that the goal of life is divine perfection or man's union with God. All our laws, our ethical codes and our forms of worship derive their value from this ultimate purpose which we have to keep in view.

D.—Father, I should like to know more about the path

which leads to this goal. What is the first thing a man has to do when he wants to start on the journey?

F.—The first thing he has to do is to turn away from all evil. As the Gītā says, vile and wicked men can never reach God. And one of the Upaniṣads says, "No one who has not turned away from bad conduct, whose senses are not under control, who is not composed and whose mind is not at peace, can obtain Him through mere knowledge." Therefore the first ascent of the upward path to God is entirely characterized by the faithful performance of one's own Dharma.

D.—What is Dharma?

F.—The word Dharma is used in our scriptures in a somewhat technical as well as a general sense. In the technical sense Dharma comprises all actions, qualities, offering, etc., which the śāstras teach us as leading to our spiritual good. In the general sense Dharma comprises all the duties that are imposed upon an individual in accordance with his position in life and with his own mental and moral development. You will see at once that the two meanings of Dharma are intimately connected together. Our duties and obligations acquire their significance only from the unseen spiritual value attached to them. And it is the function of scriptures to teach us what the spiritual value is.

D.—What do you mean by saying that Dharma in the sense of duties, is imposed on an individual in accordance with his position?

F.—Dharma takes different forms with different individuals. The duties of men differ according to their stations in life. For instance a soldier's duty is different from a doctor's. The former takes life; the latter saves it. Similarly, a master's duty is different from a servant's, a teacher's duty is different from a pupil's, a father's duty is different from a son's, and so on. The well-being of a community is secured only when the various duties of all its members are discharged in a spirit of good-will and co-operation. A house that is divided against itself will fall. Dharma therefore implies social harmony and happiness, while adharma implies social discord and misery. Our sacred books say dhāraṇāt dharmaḥ—that is, Dharma is so called because it sustains society.

D.—You have said that a man's Dharma depends not only on his station in life, but also on his mental and moral development. May I know what that means?

F.—I will explain what I mean by an illustration. Take the case of Buddha. It was his duty as a royal prince to remain in his kingdom and learn the arts of peace and war. But when a higher duty of retiring from the world to find out the cause of human misery was suggested to him by his inner voice he had to obey the call. If he had disobeyed it, he would have been false to the lights he had, and incurred sin. Thus in the case of Buddha, what was Dharma before his enlightenment would become adharma after his enlightenment.

D.—So righteousness depends not upon external acts, but upon the inward spirit of the man who acts?

F.—Quite so, my child. The Hindu scriptures often point out that inward righteousness is more important than external righteous acts and that ethical disposition is worth more than good conduct. Even our early law-givers, who insist on the formal observance of the law and the performance of rites and ceremonies, distinctly say that ethical excellence is far more important than mere ceremonial purity. For instance, Gautama says, "He who is sanctified by the forty sacraments, but whose soul is destitute of the eight good qualities, will not be united with Good, nor does he reach heaven". You should note here the contrast between sacraments which are merely ceremonies that have to be performed at the various stages of a man's life, as birth, childhood, youth, manhood, old age and death, and moral qualities such as compassion, forbearance, etc. Moreover our law-givers, in the lists that they give of penances for various sins, distinguish clearly sins of thought from sins of word and deed. The former are punished as severely as the latter

D.—Father, if, as you say, moral excellence is more important than ceremonial purity, what is the use of rites and ceremonies?

F.—The use of rites and ceremonies lies in the training they give us. They are preliminaries to moral qualities. They are never ends in themselves. They are only means to an end.

D.—What is the end?

F.—The end is the purification of the spirit. The Gītā says:— "Sacrifices, gifts and austerities purify the wise." Rites and ceremonies are the initial steps in moral progress. They are the reminders of the law. They are enjoined, not on blind authority, but with reference to the goal of life. They are intended to lead to virtues.

D.—How can rites and ceremonies lead to a virtuous life?

F.—All wisely-directed rites, when they are not simply commemorative or symbolical, have corresponding virtues in view. For instance, an offering to the gods is a rite and it is intended to lead to self-sacrifice, which is a virtue. Almsgiving is laid down as a rite, and it is intended to lead to generosity, which is a virtue. Fasting is a rite, and it is intended to lead to self-control, which is a virtue. Similarly, the five great sacrifices that a householder is enjoined to offer every day to the gods, to the ṛṣis, to the pitṛs, to men and other living beings, are intended to develop the virtues of devotion to God, devotion to learning, devotion to family, devotion to society and kindness to animals. It is only when rituals are made ends in themselves, without leading to any virtues or to any chastening of the spirit, that they become dead wood impeding the growth of the soul.

D.—But what are the chief rites and ceremonies of Hinduism?

F.—They differ from community to community and from locality to locality. So let us not go into all these details now. We are now concerned only with general principles.

D.—You say that rites and ceremonies should lead to virtues. But how do virtues help a man to reach the goal of life?

F.—A virtuous life purifies and strengthens the soul. God is eternal perfection, and to approach Him the soul must become pure. We have already seen that the end of man's life is to become divine, and that all our religious activities should be directed with reference to that end. Therefore the first ascent of the soul's upward path consists in acquiring ethical purity. The bride should put on flowers and jewels before she meets the bridegroom. Virtues are the soul's ornaments.

II

D.—What are the virtues that we have to cultivate?

F.—Almost all virtues known to man come within the province of every religion. But each religion emphasizes only a few of them, and tries to bring the rest under the one or the other of these cardinal virtues. It is the cardinal virtues emphasized by a religion that determine its individual character.

D.—What are the cardinal virtues according to Hinduism?

F.—The cardinal virtues, according to Hinduism, are amply indicated in the epics and the Purāṇas. They are exemplified in the ideal characters which all Hindus love and venerate. And, what is remarkable, they are more or less common to Hinduism, Buddhism and Jainism. Therefore they may be regarded as the distinctive marks of the religious spirit of India. They are these:— (1) purity (sattva śuddhi), (2) self-control (śama and dama), (3) detachment (vairāgya), (4) truth (satyam) and (5) non-violence (ahiṁsā).

D.—Will you please explain to me what is implied by each of these? What exactly is purity?

F.—It implies both purity of body and purity of mind. All the cleaning and washing, all the purificatory baths and ceremonies, which are enjoined by the Hindu scriptures, and the elaborate rules, which are laid down regarding food and drink, are meant to suggest purity of mind and spirit.

D.—Why should there be any rules at all for eating and drinking? How is religion concerned with these?

F.—My child, religion is not a separate activity of life. It is an influence that ought to pervade all our activities. If our aim in life is to make our souls perfect in God, anything that checks the growth of the soul should be carefully removed. Our food and drink, which sustain the physical basis of the soul, are not such unimportant things as you imagine. For instance, it cannot be a matter of indifference, from a religious point of view, whether a man drinks water or wine. So, within certain limits, it is quite necessary that there should be some general rules for the common people in these matters. Had not Hinduism in its days of vigour put its foot down on the drink habit in India, we should have had here, as in the West, the shameful spectacle of even respectable men getting drunk at times. Even among our masses, it is only after our contact with the West that the drink problem has assumed serious proportions. In the palmy days of Hindu civilization drinking was regarded as a degrading habit, and only the lowest classes indulged in it.

D.—Are there any rules then with regard to the purity of food and drink?

F.—The general rules regarding food and drink may be gathered from the following verses in the Gītā:—

"The foods that promote length of life, goodness, strength, health, happiness and cheerfulness and those that are sweet, soft, nourishing and agreeable are the favourites of the good."

"The foods that are bitter, sour, salted, over-hot, pungent, dry and burning, and that produce pain, grief and disease are liked by the passionate."

"And that which is stale and tasteless, putrid and mouldy, which is of the leavings and unclean, is the food dear to the dull."

D.—But, father, will not hard and fast rules about eating, washing and cleaning make religion a mechanical thing?

F.—Yes, they will, if a man stops with mere external purity. But the Hindu sages emphatically say that external and physical purity is intended only to lead to internal and spiritual purity. The former without the latter is, of course, worse than useless. It is only a decorated corpse.

D.—Does not inward purity mean a number of virtues?

F.—Yes. I have already said that each cardinal virtue comprises a large number of kindred virtues. Purity comprises cleanliness, straightforwardness, frankness, innocence and freedom from envy, pride and malice.

D.—Then the second cardinal virtue which you have mentioned, is self-control. What does this imply?

F.—Self-control implies the control of the flesh and the spirit. We have to root out the sins of the flesh and the sins of the mind. The latter are more subtle than the former. Sins like gluttony, drunkenness and sensuality carry their condemnation on their very faces. They attack men in all their nakedness, and their beastly nature is easily recognized. But the sins of the mind put on the guise of virtues before they attack us. Hypocrisy, pride and bigotry are easily mistaken for virtues. Generally, the masses are a prey to the sins of the flesh, and the higher classes are a prey to the sins of the mind. Self-control means the control of both body and mind. The Gītā points out how desire has for its seat the senses, the mind and the understanding. The enemy has to be fought on all these fields before he is vanquished.

D.—So self-control also implies a whole group of virtues?

F.—Yes. It implies patience, forbearance, modesty, humility, self-sacrifice and self-effacement. When a man has acquired the two cardinal virtues I have described, namely, purity and self-control, he becomes, in the language of the

Gītā, a viśuddhātmā and a vijitātmā—that is, one who has purified himself and also conquered himself.

D.—Is self-conquest the same as asceticism?

F.—Self-conquest is called asceticism when it exceeds certain limits. Some critics say that Hinduism glorifies asceticism, and that it wants its followers to suppress the flesh altogether. Hinduism does nothing of the kind. It recognizes, on the other hand, that the body is a dharma-sādhana or instrument of righteousness. Accordingly, it only seeks to regulate its appetites and cravings. The flesh is not suppressed, but is only taught its place. A man who pampers his body is not fit for the kingdom of the spirit. Hinduism takes into account all the factors of human personality—body, mind, soul and spirit—and prescribes a graded discipline for the various stages of a man's career. It lays down rules for the so-called āśramas of the student, the householder, the recluse and the sannyāsin. The householder is called upon to acquire wealth, to gratify his legitimate desires, to practise virtue and to work for salvation. The well known Hindu formula of Dharma-artha-kāma-moksa therefore indicates the ideal of complete life. It is only by slow degrees that the soul has to be weaned from the desires of the flesh. The goal of complete restraint has to be reached only in the final stage. Thus self-conquest is glorified, not for its own sake, but for the ultimate liberation of the spirit from the thraldom of the flesh. At the same time, we should not be frightened by the word asceticism. All the great men of India have been ascetics—from Buddha to Gandhi. And all Hindus, though they may not be able to live up to the ideal of a Sannyāsin, are ardent admirers of Sannyāsa.

D.—Then the third cardinal virtue, which you have mentioned, is detachment. What does that imply?

F.—Detachment is freedom from attachments or earthly ties. Every man is generally attached to his possessions, family, friends and relations, and also to his opinions—in fact, to everything which he calls his own. Naturally the attachments are very strong in early life. It is the first shock of death that opens the eyes of the inexperienced person to the ephemeral nature of these ties. When calamities happen, undisciplined minds are thrown off their balance. Some curse their fate. Some curse the gods. And some are crushed by grief. This is because they have not thought about the conditions of our tenure of life. They have not reflected on the fact that we are all creatures of time. We and the objects of our love are only like the pieces of wood that drift together for a time on the ocean flood and then part for ever. The objects of our love are given to us, so that they may be utilized for the finer issues of the soul. Everyday we see misers cut off from their hoards of wealth, tyrants from their positions of power, and all men from their nearest and dearest. Death casts its pale shadow on all our pleasures and merriments. Weak men weep and wail when they encounter the ills of life. Brave men stoically endure them and pass on. But religious men know how to meet them. Janaka, when his capital was on fire, calmly faced his calamity and said, "Mithilā is burning, but nothing that is mine perishes there". So complete was the detachment of this ideal Hindu king from his kingship. The Gītā, on almost every page, says that a man should give up all earthly ties and establish a single heavenly tie, if he is to know the bliss of God. Saṁga or earthly attachment has to give place to yoga or union with God. The former is the source of all our unhappiness, and the latter is the only guarantee of everlasting happiness.

D.—Father, I can understand detachment from our possessions being regarded as a virtue. But I cannot understand how detachment from our brothers and sisters, from our friends and relations, could be a virtue.

F.—My dear child, even our sacred domestic affections are not ends in themselves. Yājñavalkya in a famous discourse to his wife Maitreyī, in one of the Upaniṣads, says, "Verily, my dear, it is not for the love of the husband that the husband is dear, but it is for the love of the Ātman that the husband is dear. Verily, my dear, it is not for the love of the wife that the wife is dear, but it is for the love of the Ātman that the wife is dear." The pure love that our hearts learn in the family circle should be extended gradually to all. A Sannyāsin is not one who has divested himself of all love, but one who has extended his love to all, and looks upon the whole world as his family. The Gītā says:—

"He who looks upon all like himself in pleasure and pain—he is considered, O Arjuna, a perfect yogin."

Till we look upon our dearest ones as only parts of a whole, our affections are not free from the taint of selfishness. Friends come and go, but friendship remains forever. Death takes away those whom we dearly love, but it cannot take away love from our hearts. Therefore I say friendship is more real than friends, love is more real than the beloved. Love, friendship, sympathy and kindness are divine qualities; and the more we cherish them in our hearts, the nearer are we to God. And the way to cherish them is not to be blindly attached to the particular objects of those feelings. It is of course, human to love our relations and friends; but to transcend such narrow love is divine. It is a divine character, and not simply a human character that our scriptures reveal to us. Does not Rāma show a certain detachment in his love of Sītā? Did not Buddha transcend his human love of Yaśodharā and Rāhula and afterwards take them into his fold in heavenly love? So detachment does not mean the sacrifice of our affections, but their expansion and purification.

D.—You spoke of detachment from one's own opinions. What does that mean?

F.—There are many who can get over their attachment to their possessions, and their attachment to their relations and friends, but not their attachment to their opinions and prejudices—the creatures of their minds. This is the subtlest form of ahaṁkāra or egoism. A true yogin cultivates a detachment even from his own mind. He knows he ought to be above his own mind, and ought not to identify himself with even the most dearly cherished schemes of his heart. He should have detachment enough to consider all sides of a question. He should have no interests other than those of truth. And, if his inherited or acquired opinions stand between him and truth, they should unhesitatingly be brushed aside. This work would be less painful if he should cultivate the habit of detachment from the beginning.

D.—Your reply brings us to the next cardinal virtue—truth. But truthfulness is a virtue inculcated by all religions, even by those which are very primitive.

F.—Yes. In all Hindu scriptures truthfulness is constantly alluded to as the basis of both the heroic and the saintly types of character. For instance, in the Mahābhārata, Bhīṣma says to Yudhiṣṭhira:—

"It is impossible, O King, to exhaust the merits of truth. For this reason the Brāhmaṇas, the Pitṛs and the gods speak highly of truth. There is no duty higher than truth, and no sin more dreadful than untruth. Indeed truth is the very root of righteousness. Therefore we should never tamper with truth. On one occasion the merits of truth and a thousand horse-sacrifices were weighed against each other in the balance. Truth proved heavier than a thousand horse-sacrifices."

In this passage we see how the teacher passes from the ritual to the moral plane, and points out the immense superiority of the latter over the former. I have given you only one instance. But thousands of such instances can be given from our epics and Purāṇas. The colossal sacrifices made by Hariścandra, Yudhiṣṭhira and Daśaratha in keeping the promises they made show the high place given to truth by Hindu sages. In fact, our scriptures say that all virtues are only forms of truth.

D.—Therefore truth here does not mean mere truthfulness.

F.—No. It means also what is right in conduct, what is just in social relations and what is true in knowledge. I have already said that Hinduism is a progressive quest after truth. It is quest after right conduct, just dealing and true knowledge. For God is truth. He is the source of all righteousness, beauty, justice and knowledge. These are eternal values. And it is only their temporary phases that we see in the world. But sin, ugliness, injustice and ignorance are all forms of untruth, which is a mere shadow without any substance. So what our religion enjoins by satyam is not mere truthfulness, but our enthusiastic support of all correct views, just causes, right actions and beautiful ways of life. It is a virtue that opens the door to infinite progress in science, in art, in social justice and the higher morality of the future.

D.—What do you mean by the higher morality of the future?

F.—Morality is a thing of growth. In every age, our ethical codes are only partial expressions of the highest ideal revealed to us in the Veda. With reference to that ideal our codes might be extended indefinitely. Dharma, according to our sages, is not a fixed quantity. It changes from age to age. Every yuga has its own yuga-dharma. Consider, for instance, how far we have progressed from the position of our early law-givers in the matter of animal sacrifices, punishments of crimes, the treatment of the lower classes, etc.

D.—Does dharma always progress? Does it never deteriorate?

F.—Dharma deteriorates when the society becomes degenerate, or when it falls on evil times. Many of our later Purāṇas deplore that the cow of Dharma, which once walked on four legs, walked in their time only on one leg. The authors of these lived in troublous times of war and social disruption when the standard of morality went down. We have even now the heritage of those evil times. We have certainly deteriorated from the position of our early law-givers in the matter of altruism, social solidarity and the treatment of women. Dharma therefore depends for its progress on national prosperity and national independence.

D.—Is there no limit then to the progress of dharma?

F.—The progress of dharma means the progress of man towards divine perfection. Therefore who can dare prescribe limits to it? Humanity is still comparatively young. It was, so to speak, only the other day that man appeared on the earth with his notions of right and wrong. Who knows for how many millions of years the earth had rolled on its axis before man was evolved? And who knows for how many millions of years more it is going to revolve? Who knows what marvels the eternal Magician is going to produce? What was deemed impossible a thousand years ago has become possible now in the scientific world. Similarly, what is impossible now for the ordinary man in the moral sphere, owing to the weaknesses of the flesh, may become possible for the whole race a million years hence. By that time who knows but that the ascending spirit may express itself through a better instrument than human personality? Who knows but that even this globe may be peopled, before the time of its annihilation, with beings more spiritual than man?

D.—Father, what you say is rather bewildering.

F.—No, my child. I am only stating facts. Truth *is* bewildering. It is far more bewildering than our wildest imaginings. The contemplation of truth swiftly takes us away from our little systems of morals and metaphysics. The Hindu scriptures teach us that the pursuit of truth, wherever it may lead and whatever sacrifices it may involve, is indispensable to the progress of man. Hence Hinduism has never opposed scientific progress. It has never opposed speculation in metaphysics or ethics. The last page of its ethics is not yet written, and will never be written. If only we have eyes to see, a new chapter is being added to the ethics of India in our own life-time. But let me not dwell on it now. Let us pass on to the next cardinal virtue.

D.—But I should like to know what virtues you would include under truth.

F.—I would include honesty, sincerity, justice, faithfulness, a patient investigation of facts, an appreciation of all forms of beauty, and other allied virtues. In fact, as I have said our scriptures declare that all virtues are only forms of truth.

D.—Now we come to the last in our list of cardinal virtues, namely, ahiṁsā or non-violence. What does this imply?

F.—There is an oft-quoted Hindu saying—ahiṁsā paramo dharmaḥ, w' ich means that non-violence is the highest law. There is no .oubt that the gospel of non-violence is the most remarkable contribution of India to the culture of the world. Non-violence has two sides—a negative side and a positive side. On the negative side, it means refraining from giving pain to any creature in any way. And, on the positive side, it means perfect love towards all creatures. The greatest exponent of ahiṁsā in modern times thus speaks of it:—

"Non-violence is a perfect stage. It is a goal towards which all mankind moves naturally, though unconsciously. Man does not become divine even when he personifies innocence in himself. He only becomes truly a man. In our present state we are partly men and partly beasts; in our ignorance and even arrogance, we say that we truly fulfil the purpose of our species when we deliver blow for blow, and develop the measure of anger required for the purpose. We pretend to believe that retaliation is the law of our being, whereas in every scripture we find that retaliation is nowhere obligatory but only permissible. It is restraint that is obligatory. Retaliation is indulgence requiring elaborate regulating. Restraint is the law of our being. For the highest perfection is unattainable without the highest restraint. Suffering is thus the badge of the human tribe."

You know that Mahatma Gandhi, who says these words, has made the practice of non-violence a science. Non-violence has to be practised, not only by individuals, but also by communities and nations, and it has to be practised in all spheres of life. That is why I say a new chapter is being added to Hindu ethics in our own generation.

D.—Has Hinduism always taught that we should return good for evil? Or is this a comparatively new gospel?

F.—My child, scores of passages could be quoted from the Mahābhārata to show that this has been the teaching of the Hindu sages from time immemorial. Moreover, the law of love is extended in the religions that arose in India even to the sub-human world. It is not limited to humanity as in the ethical codes of other countries.

D.—But, father, is complete non-violence possible?

F.—The Hindu sages, who preach non-violence, recognize that perfect ahiṁsā is only an ideal. It is like a straight line in geometry. We can only make an approximation to it in practice. All creatures, for instance, get their food only by violence. They have to kill and eat. Some kill animal life, and some vegetable life. But, as animals are higher forms of life than vegetables, to kill animals is a greater violence than to cut vegetables. Therefore Hinduism exalts vegetarianism above meat-eating, and regards the ideal saint as one who lives on air, as it were, and who does no injury to animal or vegetable life in maintaining his bodily existence.

D.—Why does Hinduism not insist on vegetarianism?

F.—Hinduism lays down no uniform law for all sections of the community. It teaches the superiority of vegetarianism, and allows individuals and classes to reach the ideal in their own time when they have acquired the necessary adhikāra or moral competence.

D.—Then is non-violence in our country only an individual virtue or a class virtue, and not a national virtue?

F.—No, non-violence may fairly be called a national virtue in India. For, though it is practised by small sections of the society, it has considerably influenced the Hindu community as a whole. We may even say that it has made the Hindus what they are to-day. Most of their virtues and vices can be traced to the ideal of non-violence. Their mildness, their hospitality, their humanity, their horror of bloodshed, their abhorrence of taking out life, their kindness to animals and their worship of the cow are all due to the ideal of non-violence. The pacific character of Hindu civilization is a result of this ideal. It is said that the Indian masses, in spite of their terrible poverty, are far less brutal than the masses in other countries. If that is a fact, it is due to the non-violence practised by the classes.

D.—But, father, is there not another side to this picture?

F.—Yes, I have already said that most of our vices, as well as our virtues, can be traced to the ideal of non-violence. Remember ahiṁsā is only for those who are brave and strong. It is for those who can strike, but will not. To flee from the brute and the bully and call it non-violence is the worst form of self-deception. What the ideal of non-violence requires is to substitute spiritual strength for brute strength, and not cowardice for valour. When a man cannot use spiritual strength, either because he is incompetent or because his foe has no spark of humanity in him, it is his duty to use physical strength in defence of himself and what he holds dear. It is ridiculous for a lamb to cherish ideals of non-violence when the wolf is of a different opinion. So in a world, such as ours, in which men still resort to brute strength for gaining their objects, and nations compose their quarrels by means of the sword, ahiṁsā, in the hands of those who have no adhikāra for it, can only result in a lack of manliness. And a lack of manliness is the parent of many sins.

D.—What are the virtues that true ahiṁsā implies?

F.—True ahiṁsā necessarily implies gentleness, courtesy, kindness, hospitality and love. You will observe that all these are social virtues. In fact, in the list of cardinal virtues that I mentioned, all individual virtues are grouped under the first three, namely, purity, self-control and detachment; and all social virtues are grouped under the last two, namely, truth and ahiṁsā. In Hindu ethics, social virtues have a higher rank than individual virtues. And society, according to us, includes not only living men but also those who have gone before us, those who will come after us, all beings above us like the gods and the pitṛs, and all beings below us like birds and beasts. We have our duties not only to our neighbours, but also to our ancestors, to our descendants, and to all living beings lower than man. I have already pointed out to you the significance of the five great sacrifices which a householder is enjoined to offer every day. Thus we see what a grand organic conception of society the Hindu sages had. It is a conception not limited by space or time. Nor is it confined to mankind.

III

D.—Now, father, is the cultivation of all these main and subsidiary virtues the sole aim in the first stage of man's ascent to God?

F.—Yes. We begin religious life with rites and ceremonies. But these are only external means of purification. We have to pass quickly from these to virtues, which are the internal means by which the purification of the soul is effected.

D.—Has a man to progress from one virtue to another in

the order in which you have given them—purity, self-control, detachment, truth and non-violence?

F.—No. It is only for the sake of convenience that we divide and sub-divide virtues. For instance, we cannot draw a hard and fast line between individual virtues and social virtues. They are all really one, and constitute what we call a virtuous character. Their significance should always be understood with reference to the goal of religious life, namely, divine perfection. Therefore we should say that the formation of a virtuous character is the aim in the first ascent rather than the cultivation of the cardinal and other virtues.

D.—Why, what is the difference between the formation of a virtuous character and the cultivation of virtues?

F.—Virtues, like rituals, are more or less in the nature of commandments proceeding from an external authority, and only a few understand their reference to the goal of religious life. Moreover, their validity depends upon circumstances. It is not always easy to say at what point virtues cease to be virtues. Firmness easily passes into obstinacy, courage into fool-hardiness, non-violence into cowardice, self-control into self-annihilation and so on. Therefore, the cultivation of virtues may merely imply a mechanical obedience to moral commandments. This, of course, is as necessary in the beginning as are rites and ceremonies. That is why our law-givers lay down the rules of dharma in an apparently dogmatic manner. But soon the moral man has to act for himself. He has to decide for himself what is true, what is just and what is virtuous in given circumstances. He should no longer feel hampered by rules and precepts. When he has thus acquired a virtuous disposition, he becomes independent in his judgement, and rarely goes wrong.

D.—If precepts and commands are thus superseded, what is the standard to be followed?

F.—A dharmātmā or a virtuous personality is a surer standard than a rule of dharma. The former is a living tree, the latter is only a dried fruit. In the Taittirīya Upaniṣad a teacher, giving some parting advice to his pupil on the completion of his education, says, "If you should have any doubt concerning an act or a line of conduct—in such a case you should conduct yourself as teachers, who are competent to judge, capable and devoted, and who are not harsh lovers of virtue, conduct themselves."

D.—Are men the guides of right conduct, and not scripture of sacred law?

F.—Men as well as scriptures. According to Hinduism, the guides of right conduct are the scriptures, usage, the example of saints and the inner self or conscience. For Manu says, "The Vedas are the source of the sacred law, next, the Smṛti, and the conduct of those who understand the scriptures, and also the customs of holy men, and finally the satisfaction of the inner self." And Kālidāsa, in a well-known and oft-quoted verse, says that the promptings of a pure heart are a sure guide in matters of doubt. Thus, by making the example of saints an authority, and by regarding the Vedic ideal of divine perfection as the standard of reference, Hinduism keeps its dharma alive and its moral code flexible.

D.—Father, you have said that our law-givers not only lay down dharma, but also prescribe penances for various sins. What are sins? And how many of them are there?

F.—Sins, like virtues, are innumerable. Different law-givers give different lists. But they are generally classified in two ways.

D.—What are they?

F.—Firstly, all sins are divided into sins of thought, sins of word and sins of deed. For an evil thought or a harsh word is as much of the nature of sin as a wicked deed. This three-fold division shows the refinement of the Hindu ethical writers who refuse to excuse even a harsh or obscene word, though there is no evil intention behind it and though it does not result in any cruel deed.

D.—And what is the other classification?

F.—Just as we have all virtues grouped under the five cardinal virtues, so we have all sins grouped under the three deadly sins of kāma, krōdha and lōbha, or sensuality, hate and greed. The Gītā says:—

"Triple is the gate of hell, destructive of the soul—sensuality, hate and greed. Therefore one should forsake these three. The man who escapes these three gates of darkness and works for the good of his soul, reaches the supreme state."

But all divisions are rather artificial. There is only one sin, though its forms are numberless. And that is self-centered desire. Sin is simply man's opposition to God, or, more correctly, the opposition of the flesh to the spirit. A sinner is one who is out of harmony not only with the society around him, the laws of which he breaks, but also with the universal kingdom of spirit, of which he is a part. For the Dharma he is violating is only an earthly transcript of Ṛta, which the Vedas declare to be the rhythm and the order of the universe. Man, in his ajñāna or blindness, thinks that he can be independent of the rule of the universe. He is like a limb that refuses to function with the rest of the body, and sets up some local action, with the result that inflammation, pain and disease are caused. A sinner is a diseased limb of society, and a rebel against the kingdom of God. He sets his own will against that of the Creator. And, remember, both are in himself. For man is both spirit and flesh. The former is his higher nature, and the latter is his lower nature. The way of the former is jñāna or saving knowledge, and the way of the latter is kāma or ruinous desire. When Arjuna asks Kṛṣna in the Gītā what prompts a man to commit sin, he is told, "It is desire, it is wrath which springs from a passionate nature. It is a monster of appetite and sin. Know thou it is the foe here."

D.—Are all desires our foes?

F.—No. It is only unlawful desire that is the enemy. For the God of the Gītā says, "I am the kāma in all beings, when it is not opposed to Dharma". Desires are bad only when their object is the illicit gratification of the self. As long as man is self-centered and erects walls of separation between himself and his fellows, his desires come into conflict with the law of universal love and retard his progress.

D.—But how can a man of the world cease to take care of himself and his family, and act according to the law of universal love? If what you say is true, all of us are sinners.

F.—Yes. All of us are sinners in a way. Every religion teaches us that. Hindu scriptures constantly say that existence is evil, and that the Saṁsāra exists only for sinners. Buddha equates life with duḥkha. Christianity teaches that all men are born sinners, and that the world is always antagonistic to God.

D.—Is not this mere pessimism?

F.—No. For pessimism is a philosophic theory that says that life is an evil, that the world has no purpose, that nothing rules here but blind will, and that therefore men should seek deliverance from this world of misery and suffering. This is very far from Hinduism, which believes in an immanent God and the ultimate salvation of all men, and disbelieves in eternal punishment and the ultimate reality of evil. Hinduism everywhere claims to show the way to permanent happiness. It teaches that immortal souls cannot be satisfied with mortal things. Therefore it exhorts men not to put faith in the fleeting pleasures of the world, but in the joys of the spirit. There can be no beginning of religious life, unless we look upon the world as mainly evil. Dissatisfaction with the present life is the counterpart of the hope of a future life. All that most of us can do in this world is to acquire a little cleanliness in an ocean of dirt, a little righteousness in an ocean of sin, a little beauty in an ocean of ugliness and a little love in an ocean of selfishness. If we do not shrink from the dirt, the sin, the ugliness and the selfishness of the world and denounce them as evil, we have no hope of progress. We all start from a self-centered life. But when our conception of self gradually expands so as to include, not only the family but also the community and the country to which we belong, we grow less sinful. As we learn to love and work for larger units, our desires purify themselves and harmonize with the will of God. All moral progress lies in harmonizing our self-will with the Will that rules the universe.

D.—Can we get rid of our sins in this way?

F.—Yes. We can get rid of our sins most easily by expanding our souls. This creates in us a virtuous disposition and increases our spiritual power which burns up all sin. Every virtuous act, which is the outcome of our expanding love, adds to the hidden strength of the soul.

D.—Is it necessary to root out every sin from our souls?

F.—Yes, my dear. Is it not necessary to stop every leak in a ship to save it from sinking? A particular sin is only a symptom of the disease of the soul. It is not simply a local inflammation which could be removed by an external application.

D.—If that is so, what is the use of the penances and purificatory rites laid down by our law-givers?

F.—Penances and purificatory rites are prescribed only for those who have turned away from sin. They come in only after a change of heart. They are like external applications which only supplement, but can never supplant, obedience to the general laws of health.

D.—What is the use of them, if they only *follow* a change of heart?

F.—They are a mark that the man is retracing his false steps. They serve to show his repentance and his public confession. The very word prāyaścitta applied to such rites connotes a determination to change one's heart and to atone for the sin. No great law-giver ever admits that sin can be removed by means of distribution of gifts or observance of fasts and vigils without an antecedent change of heart. Penances are only confirmatory rites. They confirm the soul's purification. But the purification itself must come from within. No man can be saved from without. The health of the soul, like the health of the body, can only be evoked from within, and never be communicated from without

D.—If a man allows sin to grow in his heart and fails to purify himself, what will happen?

F.—One sin leads to another, the man's spiritual resistance becomes weak, his nature is coarsened, and he sinks low in the scale of Saṁsāra.

IV

D.—What is Saṁsāra?

F.—Saṁsāra is the cycle of births and deaths through which the soul of every creature passes before it attains Mokṣa or liberation. Hinduism teaches that all creatures as long as they are creatures, are involved in this time-process. And the state of each creature in any particular life depends upon the karma or the good and evil thoughts and deeds of its preceding lives. The law of karma is a unique and characteristic feature of the religious thought of India. It is taught not only by Hindu scriptures, but also by Buddhist and Jain scriptures.

D.—What exactly is the law of karma?

F.—The law of karma is a moral law corresponding to the physical law of causation. As a man sows, so shall he reap. Every thought and every act of his are, as it were, weighed in the scales of eternal justice. God, according to Hinduism, does not sit in judgement over human actions on some future day, but here and now. His law is wrought into our natures. Just as Nature is subject to unalterable laws, so is our moral nature also subject to law. Our characters and destinies shape themselves from life to life, not according to arbitrary commands or whims, but according to organic laws.

D.—How can the acts of a former life, which is past and gone, affect our character and destiny in this life?

F.—The acts of a former life do not die with the death of the body. They leave an indelible trace on the mind or the soul. Our scriptures call it apūrva or adṛṣṭa. This is the seed which grows into our character and destiny in the present life.

D.—Is the law of karma then one of cause and effect?

F.—Yes. It works in the moral world as the law of cause and effect works in the physical world. For instance whenever you put your hand into the fire you burn your fingers. This happens at all times and in all places. The same cause produces the same effect, provided no other cause intervenes. In fact, the cause and the effect are one. They are organically connected together. Similarly, in the moral world, whenever you steal, your character is affected for the worse. The more frequently you steal, the more thievish you become. On the other hand, whenever you help your neighbour, you improve your character. And the more frequently you help, the more beneficent you become. The law of karma is thus only an extension of the invariable sequence that we see in this life. It tells us that what we are now is the result of what we thought and did in the past, and what we shall be in the future will be the result of what we think and do now.

D.—Do you mean, then, that a man's birth and circumstances in this life depend mostly upon his own thoughts and actions in the past lives?

F.—Yes. How else can we explain the inequalities of life that we see all around us? God is not partial. He would not, of His own accord, make one man strong and another man weak, one man healthy and another man sickly, and one man sensual and another man spiritual. He would never, of His own accord, put one man in surroundings that help the progress of his soul, and another man in surroundings that hinder the progress.

D.—Father, I have read somewhere that God has made some people unhappy in this world so that there may be opportunities for others to develop the virtues of pity, compassion and love, and thus glorify Him.

F.—That cannot be right. For He must be a vain and cruel God who would make some men miserable that others might exercise their virtues on them and thus glorify Him. No, no. The inequalities of life are due to ourselves, and not to God. We carry with us our past. We *are* our own past. The mental and moral tendencies that the soul acquires in a particular life, as a result of its purposes and actions, work themselves out in suitable surroundings in the next. And new sets of tendencies are acquired, which again find a suitable environment in which they work themselves out. This process goes on through several lives till the soul obtains Mokṣa or liberation.

D.—But how is it that we do not remember anything of our past lives?

F.—Because our conscious memory, which has for its seat our brain, is stored only with the impressions acquired in this body. But, besides our conscious mind, there is a huge unexplored sub-conscious region in which is stored up all our past experience. It is this that is responsible for the working of the law of karma.

D.—Have you got any evidence for this and for the working of the law of karma?

F.—There is, first of all, what we may call the scriptural evidence. The Veda teaches it. And there are many instances in our sacred books of great Ṛṣis remembering their past lives. But, from a secular point of view, the existence of genius is the best evidence we have for the law. We often come across people who show a great genius for music, art or literature, which cannot be explained either by heredity or education or environment. Again, it often happens in the lives of many persons that a very trivial commonplace incident unlocks, as it were, a door in the heart, and a great experience that has been stored up bursts out tearing away the old landmarks and changing the man's character completely. How can such things be explained without recognizing the law of karma and admitting that we carry in our sub-conscious memory all the saṁskāras or experiences of our past lives? Even the ordinary instincts may be said to be the result of the experience acquired in past lives.

D.—Father, if we have no actual recollection of our past sins, is it just to punish us for them?

F.—What you say applies only to man-made laws and punishments, and not to natural laws and consequences. In artificial man-made laws the penalties laid down have generally no natural relation to the crimes committed. For instance, if a man steals he is either imprisoned or put in stocks or his right hand is cut off. The punishment differs in different countries, and is purely arbitrary. In such a case you may say it is unjust to punish a man for a crime of which he has no recollection. But in the case of natural law this does not apply. For instance, if a man drinks poison, he will die whether he remembers his action or not. God is not a guide sitting in a remote heaven meting out punishments according to a penal code. He is an in-dwelling spirit whose law is wrought into our natures.

D.—If a man's birth and circumstances are determined by his past karma, what is the use of his efforts now? If everything is pre-ordained for him, how can he be held responsible for his actions?

F.—Man's will is ever free. Else, moral life would be impossible. Everything is not pre-determined. Within the limits set by birth, environment and tendencies, a man has still ample scope to carve a career for himself. The Gītā in a suggestive metaphor calls the body a plot of ground. Every soul is a farmer to whom a plot of ground is given. The extent of the ground, the nature of its soil, the changes of weather to which it is exposed are all pre-determined. But the farmer is quite at liberty to till the ground, to manure it and to raise suitable crops, or to neglect it and allow it to run to waste. Similarly, there are elements of freedom, as well as elements that have been pre-determined, in the lives of all of us. The law of karma recognizes both of these.

D.—What are the elements of freedom? And what are the elements that are pre-ordained?

F.—The Hindu scriptures divide a man's karma into three parts—Prārabdha, Sañcita and Āgāmi. Prārabdha karma is that part of a man's accumulated karma which has begun to bear fruit in the present life. It is a thing which is entirely determined, and cannot be avoided. It gives rise to those conditions of a man's existence which he cannot get over, however hard he may try. We cannot, for instance, get over our sex or parentage or the colour of our skin in this life. We cannot jump out of our bodies. As far as such things are concerned, every one will admit that man is a creature of circumstances. Therefore Prārabdha karma can be exhausted only by being experienced. Sañcita karma is the name given to the accumulated karma of all the previous lives of a man. As a result of all his actions in the past, he acquires a certain character and certain tendencies. These are not unalterable like sex and parentage. It is possible to uproot evil habits by persistent effort, and plant good ones in their stead. Sañcita karma, unlike Prārabdha, can be expiated by penances. And our scriptures say that, unlike Prārabdha it can be totally destroyed by Jñāna. Lastly, Āgāmi karma is that which is being created now in the present life. Its fruits will come to us in a future life. It is entirely in our hands. As we sow, so shall we reap. If our thoughts are pure, our actions righteous, and our desires unselfish, we create for ourselves conditions which will accelerate our progress towards perfection. If, on the other hand, we sin, penal blindness overtakes us, and we go down in the normal scale of Saṁsāra, and suffer for it in the lives to come, till retributive justice brings us to our senses.

D.—Cannot all this process be completed in one life?

F.—I am surprised at your question. How many of us in this world are fit for Mokṣa, which means really God-like perfection? It is monstrous to suppose that the soul could obtain its eternal reward or its eternal punishment by the actions of a single life; for, in that case, either the reward or the punishment would be intolerably unjust. It is only after a long series of lives of sustained effort that a man could attain to the perfection of God. One span of life is all too short for the great end in view.

D.—But even one span of life is not allowed to all. Some people die young, and others live long to a very old age. How is this to be explained?

F.—I have already said that, out of the vast store of our accumulated karma, a part comes to fruition in one life. It is in accordance with this Prārabdha, that our present bodies and our surroundings have come into existence. When it is fully worked out, the soul has to depart from the body with the experience gathered here, and seek birth again elsewhere.

D.—So death is not accidental, but designed?

F.—It may seem accidental to us. But how can there be accidents in a world ruled by God, whose will is the law? One of our scriptures says, "A man will not die *before* his time has come, even though he has been pierced by a thousand shafts; he will not live *after* his time is out, even though he has been only touched by a blade of kuśa grass."

D.—If so, does not the law of karma fill us with despair that we can never avert what is sure to come to pass?

F.—But we do not know what is going to come to pass. Therein lies our incentive to work. We have to discharge our duty, and leave the result to God. If every man could interfere with the events of the world at his own will and pleasure, what a chaotic world it would be! No, no. The law of karma, far from filling us with despair, fills us with hope. It teaches us that, in the moral world as well as in the material world, nothing happens by chance. Just as a savage, who dreads a storm or an eclipse as a sign of the anger of his gods, ceases to dread it when he comes to know the laws of nature, so when we come to know the law of karma, we cease to dread the arbitrariness of chance, accident and luck. In a lawless universe our efforts would be futile. But in a realm of law, we feel secure and guide ourselves with the help of our knowledge. When we know that sin entails suffering, that we shall reap as we sow, and that our entire future will not be decided by what we do or fail to do in a single life time, but that we shall be given as many chances to improve ourselves as we want, we are filled with hope. When we know that we are the architects of our own fortunes and that it is never too late to mend, we feel strong and secure. We are glad that we are not at the mercy of a capricious God.

D.—Has God no hand then in the workings of the law of karma?

F.—You may as well ask me whether God has no hand in the workings of the laws of Nature. God works through laws. What we call a moral law or a natural law is only an embodiment of His will. At the same time, He never abdicates in favour of His law. Our scriptures call Him Karmādhyakṣaḥ—the Supervisor of the law. It is He that creates the world where each soul finds an environment suited to the tendencies it acquired in a former life. He is like the gardener who makes the seed-plots in his garden and waters them. He helps the seeds to grow; but what they grow into depends upon their own nature.

D.—Father, you said that all the inequalities of life are due to our own karma during former lives, and not to God. Did God create all souls the same in the beginning?

F.—Creation has no beginning, and souls were never created. According to our scriptures Saṁsāra is anādi or beginningless. It ever depends on God who is eternal. Even at the end of a kalpa or world-period, it exists in a subtle form in His nature.

D.—So, if the law of karma prevails for ever, can we at any time interfere with it?

F.—I am surprised at your question. The law of gravity prevails for ever. But do we not interfere with it whenever we go up a staircase? The law of karma simply states the conditions under which we have to work. It does not command us to work or not to work, any more than the law of gravity asks us to rise or to fall. Just as we erect buildings by interfering with gravity, so we can create future happiness for ourselves by "interfering" with the law of karma. I have already said that, within certain limits, we can alter our destiny even in this life.

D.—But can we alter the destiny of others also?

F.—Yes, within certain limits. If a farmer by his own exertions is able to change the quantity and the quality of his crops, he can also influence the crops of his neighbour by precept, by example and by actual help.

D.—If a man is suffering now for his bad karma in the past, why should we interfere and lessen his suffering?

F.—If it is his bad karma that brought on the suffering, it is his good karma that brings him help. We are the instruments of one another's destiny. And if we fail to help the suffering man, somebody else will help him, and we shall suffer for our hardheartedness.

D.—Is Saṁsāra then a judicial system by which every man rigorously gets his due?

F.—Not exactly. You cannot, for instance, call a family a judicial system because every child gets its due from a just and loving father, who is always ready and eager to help. It would be more correct to call Saṁsāra an educational system, where the master allows the pupils to educate themselves by seeing the natural consequences of their doings, while he is present everywhere to advise, to help and to save.

D.—How does God help us, and save us?

F.—If we surrender ourselves entirely to God, His grace can lift us away from the realm where the law of karma operates.

D.—Is there then a place where the law of karma does not operate?

F.—Yes. I said that the law operates only in the moral universe. But behind the moral universe there is a spiritual universe, where all differences are reconciled, all conflict between good and evil ceases and our sinful disposition melts away in the grace of God. There the law of karma, except for Prārabdha, has no place. For, as the physical world is subject to the law of causation, and the moral world is subject to the law of karma, so the spiritual world is subject to the law of love. The Gītā teaches us that the spiritual progress of a man lies between two types of character—a *sakta* and a *yukta*. The former is one who works from attachment to the world. The latter is one who works from attachment to God. Both of them work, and work with zeal. But there is a world of difference in their motives, and hence in the consequences of their actions. The work of the man of the world results in bondage, as all actions good and bad, when they are directed by selfish desires, bind the soul to the wheel of Saṁsāra. On the other hand, the work of the man of God results in freedom, as all actions, when they are directed by a desire to co-operate with God, set free the soul. The law of karma does not bind Īśwara, though He works incessantly for the maintenance of law and order in the universe. If we take refuge in Him and act in concert with Him in everything we do, we can escape from the realm of karma or retributive action. The Gītā says:—

"Whatsoever thou doest, whatsoever thou eatest, whatsoever thou offerest, whatsoever thou givest and whatsoever of austerities thou mayst practise—do that as an offering unto me."

"Thus shalt thou be free from the bonds of works which bear good or evil fruits. With thy mind firmly set on the way of renunciation thou shalt become free and come to me."

This kind of action is sometimes called niṣkāma karma or selfless action. It is also called karma-yoga.

D.—Is karma-yoga then opposed to the law of karma?

F.—Not exactly. The latter is the raging surf of wind and waves, while the former is the calm, deep sea. Yoga takes us away from the strife of the moral world, where the law of karma prevails, to the peace of the spiritual world, where the higher law of grace prevails.

D.—What is grace?

F.—Grace is the awakening of God in the soul. It is not something that operates from without. When we rouse ourselves to a sense of the in-dwelling God, and act in accordance with His will, we are said to be in grace. We are said to have entered the world of God.

D.—Can the grace of God wipe out our past and forgive our sins completely?

F.—When we are in grace we never mind what fruits our sins have borne. Divine forgiveness consists not in wiping out our past, but in making us indifferent to its results. We lie on the bed we have made, as others do; but we are wrapped in the love of God that protects us against all its discomforts. Great devotees of God never feel the hardships of their lot in life. In their overpowering emotion they forget all their difficulties. For, they have gained entrance into a world where, according to the Upaniṣad, "a blind man is blind no longer, a wounded man is no longer wounded, and a suffering man is no longer suffering".

D.—Can we enter that world in this life?

F.—Yes, this very moment. It is to enable us to enter that world that all this moral discipline of the first ascent, which I have described, is designed.

CHAPTER III

THE SECOND ASCENT

I

D.—Father, I have come to trouble you again with questions. This is the day on which we have to meet according to our arrangement.

F.—It is no trouble to me, my child. In talking to you I am learning more than I am teaching. In these dialogues I am, as it were, thinking aloud. We, Hindus, boast that we are a religious people. Our ethics, our sociology, our polity and our art are all based on our religious philosophy. It is religion that gives the clue to our history. But, remember, religion is not a matter of mere external observances. It is primarily a matter of conduct, knowledge and experience. Therefore it is essential that every Hindu boy and girl should know clearly the essentials of their religion. They should understand and grip the framework of steel that lies underneath our bewildering sects and rituals. If they do not do this in time, they will become prey in the end to superstition, which is the worst enemy of religion.

D.—I am glad to hear, father, that I am not troubling you. You have put me on the path of light, and I want to explore it as far as I can. I will now proceed with my questions. Last time you said that moral discipline enables us to enter the spiritual world which is subject to the law of divine love and grace. I want to know whether moral life is not enough for the liberation of man.

F.—My child, morality is not religion, any more than the gateway to a temple is the temple itself. No doubt, Hinduism insists on a man's acquiring moral purity and becoming a Dharmātma in his first ascent to God. It teaches that he who has not made himself, by strenuous endeavour, pure in thought, word and deed, and who has not acquired the necessary adhikāra or competence can never even know that there is a spiritual world. But in morality there is no finality or completeness. After every moral success we see a higher ideal which condemns once again our life of littleness and sin. Morality is like the horizon which ever recedes as we approach it. It always teaches us what we have not yet acquired, keeps us at arm's length and perpetually reminds us of our weakness. We are thus rendered helpless. And in our helplessness we crave for something which takes us out of ourselves, gives us the assurance of hope and makes us partake of a larger, purer and nobler life. This is religion.

D.—Should morality then always give place to religion?

F.—Morality always leads to true religion. And true religion always strengthens morality. When a man's religion results in or countenances an immoral practice, there is something wrong with it. Very often shady things put on the cloak of religion and stand in the way of morality. Therefore, when demands are made in the name of religion which outrage our moral sense and are inconsistent with the fundamental laws of humanity, as in the case of religious persecutions, it is religion, and not morality, that must give way. We should carefully distinguish the truly religious man from the pseudo-religious man. The latter is far inferior to a moral man. But, of course, a truly religious man is superior to a merely moral man.

D.—How is a truly religious man different from a moral man?

F.—You may as well ask me how the whole is different from the part. The moral man is like an honest mercenary, while the religious man is like an ardent patriot. Both of them fight well. But the former fights for a small gain for himself, while the latter fights for his country, forgetting himself. A merely moral life cannot give us the feeling of love, joy and exaltation and the spirit of courage and self-sacrifice which religious life gives. Mere morality cannot abolish our separateness and sin.

D.—Does religious life abolish them?

F.—It does not exactly abolish them. It renders them ineffectual. God is the perfection of purity; and by fleeing and taking refuge in Him we leave our sinful selves behind.

D.—But how can we flee to Him?

F.—That is the whole problem of the second ascent we have to discuss to-day. The first ascent, as we have seen, is in society. The complex relations of men towards one another beat all around it. But when the summit is reached and the second ascent begins, the voice of humanity dies away in the rear. You have to travel alone. You see just a little light in the darkness, and it soon fades away, and there is darkness again.

D.—Is He then at first like a fitful light?

F.—He is a constant light. It is we that are fitful. The eye of the flesh cannot see Him. And the eye of the spirit has to open itself, and acquire steadiness of gaze.

D.—But how is this done?

F.—It is done by means of prayer, contemplation and love—in a word, by bhakti.

D.—What exactly is bhakti?

F.—A great Hindu devotee—the author of the Nārada-Sūtras—defines bhakti as an intense love of God, and says:—"A man who loves God has no wants nor sorrows. He neither hates nor rejoices, nor strives with zeal for any ends of his own. For through bhakti is he moved to rapture, and through bhakti does he attain peace, and is ever happy in spirit." The author goes on to describe bhakti as an "experience pure and selfless, subtle, unbroken and ever-expanding. A man, who has once experienced it, will see that alone, hear that alone and speak that alone, for he ever thinks of that alone."

D.—Does God respond to this intense feeling?

F.—Yes. The prasāda or the grace of God is God's response to man's bhakti. All great Hindu saints teach us that, as sure as day follows night, grace follows the yearning of faith. The author I have quoted just now says, "Worship God at all times with all your heart, and with all your mind. Glory him in your heart, and He will soon reveal Himself to you, and you will feel His presence." And Kṛṣṇa says in the Gītā "To those that are devoted to me and worship me do I give the steady mind by which they come to me. Out of compassion for them do I dwell in their hearts and dispel the darkness born of ignorance by the shining lamp of wisdom."

D.—You say that God reveals Himself to the worshipper. May I know how exactly He reveals Himself?

F.—He takes on the form you have chosen to worship. Kṛṣṇa says in the Gītā: "Howsoever men approach me, even so do I accept them." If you worship Him as Nārāyaṇa, He will come to you as Nārāyaṇa. If you worship Him as Śiva, He will come to you as Śiva. If you worship Him as Devi, He will come to you as Devi. Or if you choose to worship any of the Avatār forms, He will reveal Himself as such to the eye of your mind. To Tulasi Das He appeared as Rāma, to Caitanya He appeared as Kṛṣṇa and to Śri Rāmakṛṣṇa He appeared as the mother Kālī. The Gītā says, "Whatever be the form which a devotee seeks to worship with faith, I make his faith steadfast in that form alone."

D.—Is not Nārāyaṇa separate from Śiva? Are not Brahmā, Viṣṇu and Śiva subordinate to the Great God Nārāyaṇa?

F.—No, my child. There is only one God. The Vedas describe Him by the neuter noun Brahman, for in Godhead there are no distinctions of sex. Sometimes He is simply called "That", for no human description can ever do justice to His infinitude. Brahman in relation to the universe is called Īśwara; and Īśwara is termed Brahmā when He creates, Viṣṇu when he protects, and Rudra when he destroys. These names only denote the different aspects of the one God. That is why they are called the Trimūrti—the One with three forms. The Viṣṇu Purāna says, "The one only God, Janārdana, gets the designation of Brahmā, Viṣṇu and Śiva according as He creates, preserves or destroys." Of course, in popular religion these became separate gods with appropriate symbols, dwelling-places, vāhanas or vehicles and followers. The abstract ideas regarding the three different aspects of God were thus rendered concrete to the masses. At one time it was all a living symbolism.

D.—What is the symbolism of Brahmā, Viṣṇu and Śiva having consorts of their own?

F.—A little thinking will make that clear to you. We have already seen that the supreme Īśwara has the power of creating, preserving and destroying the world. This power is inseparable from God. As the sunlight is inseparable from the sun, as the power to burn is inseparable from fire, so is Śakti or the creative, protective and destructive power inseparable from God the creator, protector and destroyer. Therefore in popular religion it is personified and represented as the consort of Īśwara. An important and widespread school of Hinduism in Northern India worships Śakti as the Mother of the universe. Śakti is simply the active aspect of Īśwara engaged in the creation, protection and destruction of the world. As Saraswatī, she is the wisdom and the art of God. As Lakṣmī, she is the grace of God that brings prosperity and happiness to some, and salvation to others. And as Umā, she is the virginal purity of mountains and forests. The Devī-Bhāgavata describes her as sporting at the time of the dissolution of the world, hiding within herself the types of all things.

D.—Is it not very confusing to have the powers and functions of the one God thus divided and sub-divided and personified?

F.—Well, I don't know. Do you think it is very confusing to call the ocean that surrounds our country by various names, as the Bay of Bengal, the Arabian Sea and the Indian ocean—not to speak of the Palk Strait, the Gulf of Cambay, etc.? You should remember that Hinduism was developed under very complex conditions. Even in a small homogeneous community it is difficult to find a uniform religious formula that would satisfy the needs of all minds. What satisfies the young may not satisfy the old. What satisfies the labourer may not satisfy the scholar. It is nothing short of violence to thrust all minds into the pigeon-hole of a single formula. The difficulty is increased a thousand-fold when the community is spread over a vast continent, and includes different races with varying levels of culture. Every one of the races that come within the fold of Hinduism had its own gods, its own rites and ceremonies and its own methods of worship. Hinduism had the difficult task of reconciling all these and finding their greatest common measure. But, fortunately, the formula that had already been discovered by the Vedic sages, namely, "Ekam sad, viprā bahudhā vadanti" was elastic enough to admit any number of gods into the Hindu Pantheon, without doing violence to the deepest spiritual intuitions of the Aryan race. It is marvellous how, amidst the conflicting claims of various tribal deities and the clashing interests of different religious units and the confusing details of local customs and ceremonies, the integrity of the philosophy of the Upaniṣads is maintained. Out of the process of assimilation that went on for centuries in the Hindu fold we have developed two characteristically Hindu doctrines, of Iṣṭa-Devatā and of Adhikāra.

D.—What is the doctrine of Iṣṭa-Devatā?

F.—Out of the numerous forms of God conceived in the past by the heart of man and recorded in our scriptures the worshipper is taught to choose one which satisfies his spiritual longing and make that the object of his adoration and love. This is his Iṣṭa-Devatā. It may be one of the Trimūrti, or one of the Avatārs or one of the myriad forms of Śakti. Or it may even be a local or tribal deity rendered concrete to the eye of the flesh by means of an idol.

D.—Father, is not idolatry a crude method of worship?

F.—It is wrong to call the Hindu worship of images idolatry. For Hindu scriptures do not say that the image that is recommended for worship is God. A well-known passage in one of the Upaniṣads says, on the other hand, "Of Him whose name is Great Glory there can be no image." Our scriptures clearly say that the pratīka or the substitute is not God, but only a means of making the mind dwell on God. They point out that in this kind of upāsanā or worship, God is the object of worship, and that He is superimposed on the Pratīka for the time being. He is duly invoked, superimposed and worshipped by means of the sixteen ritual acts (ṣoḍaśa upacāra) and restored again at the end to His true place in the heart. This method of worship is therefore recommended for the purpose of making one's devotion definite. An idol serves the same purpose to the common people as a flag does to an army. It focusses men's devotions, as a flag focusses men's martial valour. At the same time, Hinduism clearly lays down that mental worship is superior to the worship of images. But it must be admitted that all worship is at bottom idol-worship. Every form with which we invest the Formless is an idol. The primitive man makes a scrawl of a head and arms on a piece of stone, and calls it God. The civilized man shuts his eyes and imagines a person with head and arms, and calls him God. Both are idols. The difference is not one of kind, but only one of degree. Hinduism has the courage to say so. And it has also the humanity to admit within its fold even those who cannot rise above grossly concrete forms of God.

D.—Father, why are the forms of our gods and goddesses generally so unnatural with many arms and many heads?

F.—My dear, this is too big a question. To answer it I have to explain to you the ideals of Indian art. And the subject may lead us far beyond our present purpose.

D.—But I am anxious to know it, father. Can you not explain it briefly?

F.—Yes. I will explain it. But I must be very brief. Hindu art is quite different from Greek art which gives us such wonderful figures of physical beauty. The former at its best, is ideal, social and hieratic. You should clearly understand these three terms. Firstly, it is ideal because it never cares to imitate the objects of the world, but aims at representing ideal figures and ideal forms. It reverses the common maxim that art is an imitation of life. It believes, on the other hand, that life should be an imitation of art. The Hindu artist, whether he is a sculptor or a painter, represents the ideal world to which the actual world has to transform itself. He gives concrete shape to the noble and gracious characters that the epic poet has conceived. He reveals to the eye of the flesh the transfigured nature which the yogin sees in a vision. He is not concerned with the sordid details of everyday life, but with the great actions of the gods or the mighty forces of evil that involve the fortunes of a world. His art is not therefore pretty or imitative. It is not realistic or naturalistic. We have no doubt some fine specimens of naturalistic art belonging to the early Buddhist period. But they do not represent the highest phase of Indian art. Secondly, our art is social, not individualistic. The conception of a separate individual self belongs to a lower order of reality, according to Hindu religious belief. Individuality, self-assertion and self-expression are, according to us, signs of immaturity. The Hindu artist is accordingly concerned only with the ideals which tradition has handed down and which his community believes in. He carefully suppresses his own individual notions, idiosyncrasies and eccentricities. He speaks in a language which is known to all. He employs a symbolism, the key to which is in the possession of every member of the community. His genius is measured by the clearness, the ease and the adequacy with which he expresses in his medium the deepest aspirations of his people. His originality lies only in the transparency of his art, which is therefore classical in the best sense of the term. Thirdly, Hindu art is a hieratic art, because in its best moments it has always subserved a religious purpose. It has been the hand-maid of religion. Its symbolism is therefore the symbolism of our scriptures.

D.—What are the best specimens of Indian art that show these qualities you have described?

F.—The great compositions that are found in the cave temples of Bādāmi, Ellora and Elephanta and the sculptural reliefs of Māmallapuram fully illustrate the features of Indian art that I have mentioned. The dance of Śiva, the slaying of Hiraṇyakaśipu by Narasiṁha, the shaking of Kailāsa by Rāvaṇa, the killing of Mahiṣāsura byDurgā, and the penance of Arjuna are represented in them. They are not events that take place on the human plane. They are symbolic of the great cosmic forces, terrific or beneficial, in comparison with which man and his little world sink into nothing. In such compositions there is little room for naturalism or prettiness or anatomical correctness or a delicate sense of proportion. What the critic has to pay attention to is the energy, the feeling, the expression, the bold imagination and the underlying idea. We have here colossal forms of good and evil, beauty and ugliness. Monstrous and terrific figures occupy the stage as much as grand and noble ones. Until we enter into the idea of each piece we are likely to regard many of the forms in it as hideous and repulsive. But when once we place ourselves in the position of the artists and the congregations of the faithful for whom they were intended, we begin to see the lofty design and the grand purpose of these works of art, which, by their very nature, do not admit of artistic perfection. What applies to these great marbles applies to many, though not all, of the images in our temples.

II

D.—Father, you made mention of two characteristically Hindu doctrines—that of Iṣṭa-Devatā and that of Adhikāra. You have explained the first. We now come to the second. What is the doctrine of Adhikāra? You have frequently used that word in these dialogues in the sense of moral competence. Am I right?

F.—Yes. Moral and spiritual competence. The doctrine of Adhikāra means that an ideal teacher should adapt his teaching to the needs of his pupil. It is worse than useless to teach abstract philosophy to a man whose mind hungers for concrete gods. A labourer may require a type of religion different from that of the scholar. So instruction should be carefully graded. The skill of the teacher consists in discovering the next step which his pupil can take, and making him concentrate on that, and not wasting his time on vague and abstract ideas. Thus he should lead him step by step.

D.—Does Hinduism then insist on a progressive bhakti?

F.—Yes. Kṛṣṇa says in the Gītā, "Even those devotees who worship the other gods with faith worship Me alone, O Arjunạ, but by the wrong method. I am, indeed, the Lord and the enjoyer of all sacrifices but because they do not know Me in truth they fall." Again, "The ignorant regard Me, the unmanifested, as having manifestation. They do not know My supreme nature, the immutable and the transcendental." Accordingly, Hindu scriptures describe various degrees and forms of bhakti.

D.—What are the degrees of bhakti?

F.—First of all, there is the broad division of bhakti into lower bhakti and higher bhakti—aparā-bhakti and parā-bhakti. The latter need not concern us now. For it consists of meditation on the formless and unmanifested Brahman, which is recommended for a man who has finished the second ascent that we are now considering. It is the highest kind of bhakti of which only a few are capable. The Gītā says, "The difficulty of those whose minds are set on the unmanifested is greater. For the path of the unmanifested is hard for the embodied to reach." The God of love is not the Absolute described as Sat-Cit-Ānanda by the philosopher, but Īśwara, the highest manifestation of that Absolute vouchsafed to the human spirit. For bhakti takes the path of least resistance and sails smoothly along the human currents of love and friendship, and carries us safe to the haven of God.

D.—So contemplation on the unmanifested Brahman is parā-bhakti, and the love of the manifested Īśwara is aparā bhakti?

F.—Yes. Aparā-bhakti or Gauṇī-bhakti is theistic faith. It assumes that the ultimate source of all things is a single supreme Personality, who being perfect in every way, should be the object of our love and adoration, and who responds with His grace to our prayers. And there are several degrees in this type of bhakti. Śrīdhara, the learned commentator of the Bhāgavata-purāṇa, says that there are as many as eighty-one degrees. But for all practical purposes, it is enough if we recognize three degrees—bāhya-bhakti, ananya-bhakti and ekānta-bhakti.

D.—What is bāhya-bhakti?

F.—Bāhya-bhakti, as the word itself indicates, is external bhakti. It is the adoration paid to something outside ourselves. It is based on the unenlightened (tāmasa) feeling that God is external to us, and that He dwells in a particular locality—a temple, a shrine or a holy bathing ghat. Our pilgrimages, our worship of images, symbols and sacred books are all examples of bāhya-bhakti. Popular religion does not generally rise above this level.

D.—What is ananya-bhakti?

F.—Ananya means, "not another". Ananya-bhakti, therefore, is the exclusive and passionate (rajasa) worship of one's Iṣṭa-Devatā in the heart. It is an intense monotheism. It clears the mind of the worshipper of many cobwebs of superstition, and gives a healthy direction to the spirit of devotion. To understand the purity and the beauty of monotheistic faith in the Hindu fold one should read the great Rāmāyana of Tulasi Das. But the danger of this type of bhakti is that it may give rise to bigotry and cruelty towards those who have different conceptions of God and different methods of approach. It must, however, be said that the Hindu ananya-bhakti has rarely resulted in intolerance or iconoclastic zeal or religious massacres. The Hindu monotheist has always recognized that the gods whom others worship are only different forms of his own Iṣṭa-Devatā.

D.—And what is ekānta-bhakti?

F.—Ekānta-bhakti is the purest (sāttvika) type of bhakti, for here the worshipper loves God for His own sake and not for his gifts. In the other two types God is worshipped generally for the sake of the gifts, not necessarily material, that come in the wake of His grace. When we suffer from want, when we are in pain and sorrow and when death snatches away our dear ones, we naturally fly to Him for refuge and pray for comfort and consolation. The divine Helper is always at hand waiting patiently. The peace He brings to us, when once He is allowed to come into our hearts, is so great that we gradually learn to crave for Him alone at all times, in prosperity as well as adversity. In fact, when He comes to dwell in us we become indifferent to external prosperity and adversity, His presence is our prosperity, and His absence our greatest adversity. When He is present we can tide over every difficulty. But when He withdraws Himself, as He often does even from His greatest bhaktas, we fall from the heights of illumination and creep along the miserable ways of routine and sin. In such periods of darkness we have to hold our souls in patience, faithfully discharge our duties and pray in solitude, as fervently as our heavy hearts allow us to do, for the home-coming of the departed One. The author of the Nārada-Sūtras rightly points out that the mark of true bhakti is the consecration of all actions to Him and a feeling of anguish when His presence is withdrawn. He also gives us the following description of ekānta-bhaktas. "They ever converse with one another of their love with choking voice, with tears in their eyes and with a thrill in their bodies. Purified are the families of such men, and purified is their land. They make holy places holier, righteous actions more righteous and sacred books more sacred. For they are filled with His spirit. At their love the spirits of their forefathers rejoice, the gods dance, and the earth feels secure. There is no distinction among them of caste or culture, beauty or rank, wealth or profession. For His are they all." In a word, ekānta-bhaktas are those who are mad after God. They are dead to the world. They live and move in a radiant world of their own where all things are transfigured by a mystic light into the forms of the Divine Spirit. Hence they see all things in God, and God in all things. They feel the uncreated light in the heart

D.—You spoke of the forms as well as the degrees of bhakti. Now, what are the forms of bhakti?

F.—Bhakti, which is the feeling of the worshipper towards the worshipped, has a variety of forms, when interpreted in terms of human relationship. Hindu bhakti-śāstras describe nineteen different forms of bhakti of which the most important are five.

D.—What are they?

F.—When God is conceived as a person, the feeling of the worshipper towards Him may be that of the servant to the master, as in the case of Hanumān in the Rāmāyaṇa. Such a type of bhakti is called Dāsya-bhāva. Or it may be that of the friend to the friend, as in the case of Sudāma in the Bhāgavata-purāṇa. Such a type of bhakti is called Sakhya-bhāva. Or it may be that of the parent to the child, as in the case of Yaśoda, the foster-mother of Kṛṣṇa. Such a type of bhakti is called Vātsalya-bhāva. Or it may be that of the wife to the husband, as in the case of Sītā or Rukmiṇī. Such a type of bhakti is called Kānta-bhāva. Or, finally, it may be the romantic love of the beloved to the lover, as in the case of the Gopīs like Rādhā towards Kṛṣṇa. Such a type of bhakti is known as Madhura-bhāva. A synthesis of all the nineteen types of bhakti is known as Mahābhāva. Indeed, love of God is like an ocean. And there are as many forms of it as there are gulfs and bays in an ocean. Theoretically, each bhakta has his own form of bhakti, as each man sees his own rainbow. But he should take care that his bhakti should be free from the inevitable limitations of the form.

D.—What do you mean by the limitations of the form?

F.—What I mean is that Dāsya-bhāva, which resembles the love of the servant to the master, should not degenerate into servility. Sakhya-bhāva, which resembles the love of friends to one another, should not degenerate into familiarity. Vātsalya-bhāva, which resembles the love of parents to children should not degenerate into sentimentality. Kānta-bhāva, which resembles the love of a wife to her husband, should not degenerate into domesticity. And finally Madhura-bhāva, which resembles the love of the beloved to the lover, should not degenerate into sensuality. It should not be forgotten that we are all spirits that have sprung from God, as sparks from a central fire, and that we are seeking to reunite with Him—each in his own way. Though the spirit has to accept the limitations of the flesh and work within those limitations, it should never be unmindful of its own essential purity and freedom.

III

D.—But do our Bhakti-Śāstras give any practical guidance to those who earnestly desire to lead a spiritual life?

F.—Yes. They not only analyze, as we have seen, the

forms and degrees of bhakti, but also describes the ways and means of bhakti, and undertake to guide us to the feet of God.

D.—What are the ways and means?

F.—First of all they are divided into Bahira.nga Sādhana or external means and Antara.nga Sādhana or internal means.

D.—What are the external means?

F.—To this class belong offerings, vows, prostrations, reading sacred books, chanting hymns, repeating the Holy Name and seeking the grace of a Guru.

D.—What is repeating the Holy Name?

F.—In the later Bhakti schools of Rāmānanda, Tulasi Dās, Vallabha, Nānak and Caitanya, repeating the name of the Lord and seeking His grace through that of Guru are considered of very great importance. The name of the Lord (Satnām or Rāmnām) is said to be as important as His form. The mystic utterance is the mediator between God and man. It is a revelation in speech of the unspeakable and the uncreated. Therefore meditation on the name is calculated to fill the soul with devotion. Similarly, the Guru is the mediator. He guides us in the ways of the Lord. Without a wise spiritual director who has trodden the paths himself and who knows the needs of our souls, it is difficult for us to reach our goal. Books and scholars make us only know about God. But a true Guru makes us know Him indeed through his own direct experience. His grace is therefore essential at the outset. It is the most potent of the external means.

D.—And what are the internal means?

F.—The internal means are, mainly, renunciation (vairāgya), knowledge (jñāna) and the practice of yoga.

D.—Will you please explain these to me in detail? How does renunciation help bhakti?

F.—If bhakti or devotion is to result in supreme happiness, which the devotee feels when he lives in grace in the sight of his Lord, he has to pay a heavy price for it. God demands the highest sacrifice a devotee can offer. Though it is not necessary that a devotee should formally renounce the world, his internal renunciation should be real and final. He should become thoroughly dead to the world before he can become fully alive to God. We often resign, but with limitations. We often renounce, but with exceptions. We try to please God, but we also try to please men. Our hearts are lifted up to heaven, but they are not free from earthly taint. That is why so few of us are illumined.

D.—But how can a man renounce all things before approaching God?

F.—It is not necessary to begin with renouncing all things. I have only said that the highest bhakti demands complete renunciation. As a matter of fact, bhakti itself helps one in renouncing earthly pleasures. The Gītā says, "The objects of sense fall away from the soul in the body when it ceases to feed on them, but the taste for them is left behind. Even the taste falls away when the Supreme is seen." Love of God and renunciation of the world act and react upon each other. Moreover, it is not so much our renouncing worldly things that matters, as our despising them in our hearts. For, as the Nārada-Sūtras say, eat and drink we must as long as we are in the flesh. Only we should not indulge in these things or pay more attention to them than is necessary. Every progressive devotee should therefore measure his love of God by his renunciation of the worldly spirit. Of course, this does not mean that he should leave his post of duty, unless he feels a higher call. On the other hand, it means that he should discharge that duty as a loyal servant of God in a spirit of self-sacrifice and with no desire for any earthly reward. For no offering is so pleasing to God as our hard, efficient, unrecognized and unrequited labour at the post to which He has called us.

D.—Next to renunciation you mentioned jñāna among the internal means. What exactly do you mean by jñāna? I have heard that jñāna is superior to bhakti.

F.—It is idle to dispute whether jñāna is subsidiary to bhakti, or bhakti is subsidiary to jñāna. It all depends upon the meaning we give to these words. I have used the word jñāna here in the sense of mere religious knowledge. There is a higher jñāna and a lower jñāna, as there is a higher bhakti and a lower bhakti. The higher jñāna is not different from the higher bhakti. The lower jñāna is the complement of the lower bhakti. Therefore it is included among the internal means of bhakti. We have already seen that Hinduism insists on progressive bhakti. It expects us to proceed from bāhya-bhakti to ananya-bhakti, and thence to ekānta-bhakti and finally to parā-bhakti. While preaching toleration towards all types of bhakti, Hindu scriptures never encourage mūḍha-bhakti or blind faith. A devotee, on the other hand, is expected to have an open mind and ever pray for light, so that he may possess more and more adequate conceptions of God. He should never forget that every human conception of God is imperfect. Therefore he should ceaselessly try to make his own conception more and more perfect. For this purpose it is necessary that he should carefully read the religious literature of his country and the great scriptures of the world, and keep himself abreast of the religious thought of his generation. But there is a danger here.

D.—What is it?

F.—Many people are apt to think that mere religious knowledge will save them. Religious knowledge is one thing, and religious experience is another. It is quite possible that you may learn all the technicalities of the Vedānta philosophy without ever possessing any spirituality. You may be an eminent theologian explaining to a wondering multitude all the secrets of the kingdom of God. But if your heart has never been visited by the Divine Person, you are only a spy in the kingdom, and not a loyal citizen. If you have only religious knowledge, you are like a man who has only one leg. With one leg you cannot even stand steady. Much less, therefore, can you walk to your goal.

D.—And now, lastly, what is yoga? And how is it a means to bhakti?

F.—The word 'yoga' is used in several different senses in our scriptures. It is used in the sense of power, prosperity, rule, devotion, endeavour, union and so on. The word literally means 'yoking'. In fact 'yoga' and 'yoke' are etymologically one and the same word. Therefore yoga is used in the sense of union in the Upaniṣads and the Bhagavad-Gītā. As all our sin and misery are due to our separation from God, we must come back to Him and be in union with Him if we want to have permanent happiness. This union is to be effected through disinterested action (karma-yoga), through loving devotion (bhakti-yoga) and through spiritual insight (jñāna-yoga). But 'yoga', in a technical sense, is used to indicate not the goal of religious life, but the way. Patañjali, the author of the 'Yoga-sūtras' was the first to systematize the practices of this technical yoga. He defined yoga as *Citta vṛtti nirodha* or restraining the functions of the mind. But the practices themselves had been in vogue in this country since the Vedic period. The Upaniṣads mention them. The Buddhist and Jaina scriptures approve of them and prescribe them. The Bhagavad Gītā recommends them. Therefore all our later bhakti scriptures accept them as a legitimate means of concentrating our minds on God. Thus there is practical unanimity on the part of all Indian teachers of religion as to the utility of yoga practices.

D.—But what are yoga practices?

F.—Yoga is described as aṣṭāṅga or having eight accessories. Therefore we have eight kinds of mental discipline, namely, yama, niyama, āsana, prāṇāyāma, pratyāhāra, dhāraṇa, dhyāna and samādhi.

D.—Will you please explain these terms?

F.—I will explain briefly what they indicate. For details you will have to read technical books on the subject. The first two, yama and niyama, indicate the preliminary ethical preparation necessary for a yogin. Yama is abstention. The sādhaka or the student should abstain from slaughter, falsehood, theft, incontinence and possession of property. Of these abstentions the most important is the first. All virtues are rooted in ahiṁsā or non-violence. But, as we have already discussed this cardinal virtue and all that it implies, we may pass on to the next, discipline—niyama.

D.—What is niyama?

F.—Niyama is observance. It comprises purity (both internal and external), contentment, austerity, study of sacred texts and prayer to God. But these also we have already discussed under cardinal virtues and the other means of bhakti. Thus yama and niyama—abstention and observance—are intended for the moral training of the sādhaka. Then the next three—āsana, prāṇāyāma and pratyāhāra—are also preliminary accessories to yoga.

D.—What do these words mean?

F.—Āsana is the posture suitable for meditation. It is a physical help to concentration. After the preliminary moral training, a man should sit down in a convenient posture before he can concentrate his mind. Pataænjali defines āsana simply as the posture which is steady and comfortable—*Sthirasukhamāsanam*. Then the sādhaka should practise prānāyāma or regulation of breath. This consists of prolonged expiration (recaka), inspiration (pūraka) and retention and (kumbhaka) of breath. But these exercises have to be done under the proper guidance of a Guru. Else they may lead to danger.

D.—But what is the use of prāṇāyāma?

F.—Prāṇāyāma is very beneficial to health, apart from its being a means to concentration. Respiratory exercises clear the lungs, steady the heart, purify the blood and tone up the whole nervous system. The yoga system realizes that the body is not a thing apart from the spirit, but its instrument and expression. Therefore it aims at perfecting the body, as well as the mind and the spirit. There is a false notion among some people that yoga aims at torturing the body. Far from doing so, yoga tries to produce kāyasampat or perfection of the body, which is said to consist in "beauty, grace, strength and the compactness of a thunderbolt". Prāṇāyāma also produces serenity of mind, which is very essential to contemplation.

D.—Then what is Pratyāhāra?

F.—Pratyāhāra is retraction or withdrawing the senses from their corresponding outward objects. That is, the mind is to be shut against all impressions from the outside world. If this is done, it ceases to be affected by external influences. By these practices, the sādhaka qualifies himself for contemplation. He has brought his body, his senses and his mind thoroughly under control. He is now fit to enter on the higher phase called Rāja-yoga comprising the last three acts of discipline—dhāraṇa, dhyāna and samādhi.

D.—What is dhāraṇa?

F.—Dhāraṇa is the fixing of the mind on any particular object. It is concentration. The sādhaka should concentrate his mind on some physical point or on the light in his own heart or on the form of his Iṣṭa-devatā so as to gain perfect steadfastness. The mind thus concentrated passes on to dhyāna or meditation, which is defined as an uninterrupted flow of thought towards the object of devotion. Dhyāna results finally in samādhi in which all self-consciousness is lost and only the object of meditation shines forth. The mind loses its sense of identity and assumes the form of the object which it contemplates. Two degrees are recognized in samādhi—conscious samādhi and superconscious samādhi. In the former the object meditated on is still distinct from the meditating subject, in the latter this distinction disappears. We are told that in the state of conscious samādhi the yogin attains marvellous supernormal powers (siddhis) of clairvoyance and clairaudience, of thought-reading and thought-transmission and of knowing the past and the future. But the Yoga-Śāstra clearly points out that these supernormal powers are really obstacles in the way of samādhi. It is only by disregarding them and passing on that the yogin reaches his goal of union with God. Thus the yoga discipline, which aims at the purification of the body and the training of the mind in concentration, is a means to the vision of God.

D.—Father, is it necessary that one should have recourse to all these ways and means of bhakti you have now described?

F.—My child, it is only for purposes of instruction that we divide and sub-divide the sādhanas, as we divide and sub-divide virtues. Moral life is one, and so is religious life. There is only one way, as there is only one God. But there are several stages in it, and hence we have several names. All of them are more or less arbitrary and exist only in theory. Begin to lead a religious life, and you will be able, from your own experience, to add to or subtract from the lists of sādhanas given by the old masters. It is the spirit behind their instruction that we have to imbibe, and not the minute and indistinguishable details. The author of the Śāṇdilya-Sūtras; after admitting that the subsidiary forms of devotion have to be adapted according to time and necessity, plainly says "Īśware tuṣṭe ekopi balī," that is, when God is pleased even one of the means is effectual. Therefore there is only one thing that is indispensable, and that is the grace of the Lord. You may practise all the external sādhanas and all the internal sādhanas without exception, you may steep yourself in religious literature and you may acquire the reputation of being a pious man. But all this is of no avail without the grace of God. There is an oft-quoted verse in the

Upaniṣads which runs thus: "Not by study, not by intelligence and not by much learning is this Ātman to be obtained. It can be obtained only by him whom It chooses. To such a one the Ātman reveals its true nature." This does not mean that grace is capricious. It only means that God is a searcher of hearts. We can deceive the world, we can deceive ourselves, but we can never deceive Him. He sees through all our studies, our clever arguments and our pious poses. He sees what sincerity there is in our hearts, and sends His grace accordingly.

D.—So the grace of God depends entirely on man's sincere effort?

F.—Well, there is difference of opinion among Hindu theistic teachers on this point. Some hold that man's bhakti has to co-operate with God's grace for salvation, as the young of the monkey have to make an effort and hold on to their mother, as she carries them over the branches of trees. But others hold that the grace of God is all-powerful and operates even without man's endeavour, as the cat carries its young from house to house without any effort on their part. The latter view has given rise to the doctrine of prapatti.

D.—What is prapatti?

F.—Prapatti means taking refuge. According to this doctrine, man has only to throw himself on the mercy of God for salvation. It is idle to think of his own good works and knowledge as his qualifications. For, what are they compared with his sins, and his ignorance? The overwhelming sense of the littleness of man, compared with the ineffable perfections of God, makes the worshipper exclaim, "I have taken refuge in Thee. Sinful and miserable as I am, be pleased to pick me up from the dust and set me up in Thy presence". To all such worshippers the Bhagavān of the Gītā, in a grand utterance, makes the following reply:—

"Renounce every rule of life and come unto Me alone for shelter. Sorrow not. I will release thee from all sins."

In another place He says:—

"Having fixed thy thoughts on Me, thou shalt surmount every obstacle by My grace. But if from self-conceit thou wilt not listen, thou shalt utterly perish."

IV

D.—In the verse you have just now quoted it is said that a devotee can surmount every obstacle by the grace of God. What are the obstacles in the way of a devotee?

F.—A devotee has, of course, the usual difficulties in life which all men have as a result of disease, bereavement, adverse circumstances, unsatisfied desires, conflict of duties and a thousand other things. But not all of them are obstacles in his path. Some of them may even help him. For, adversity keeps the soul awake, while prosperity often sends it to sleep.

D.—What then are the real obstacles?

F.—The real obstacles are of his own making. There is no recognized list of them. But we can get an idea of them from the numerous 'Lives of Saints' in our epics and purāṇas. They are mainly three—vanity, extravagance and loss of faith.

D.—How can vanity stand in the way of a devotee who has renounced all earthly ambitions?

F.—When a man ceases to be vain about his earthly possessions, and begins to lead a religious life, he is generally tempted to be vain about his spirituality. When he ceases to look down on his poorer neighbours and tries to be religious, he begins to look down on those who are less religious than himself. He waxes indignant over the sins of others. He becomes harsh and intolerant. He becomes a moral pedant, a self-constituted censor, and a pitiless judge of men. Or, again, he is tempted to make a parade of his religiosity. He becomes anxious that his devotions should be known to all. He is pleased with the reputation he gets for spirituality, and is displeased when others do not recognize his merit. All this is not real religion, but only playing at religion. Alas, many a youthful saint indulges in this kind of play. It will never do. If we want to have the grace of God, we must leave the limelight, we must step out of the theatre altogether, not through vanity and pride, but through boundless humility and perfect charity; then will the grace of God come to us. A true bhakta should be prepared to be ignored and despised. He should practise his devotions in secret, and should rather appear far less religious than he really is. He should never claim any respect or precedence for himself, but sit among the poor and the lowly. He should never draw attention to himself by any odd or eccentric ways. He should conduct himself as other men do. He should ever speak of all with great charity, dwelling on their virtues and ignoring their weaknesses. He should be hard on himself, pitiless towards himself and angry with himself. But he should be gentle, kind and forgiving towards others. He should always endeavour to make himself pure, and others happy. And he should do all this with perfect naturalness and ease, and not as one who wishes to parade his humility and charity. For spiritual pride, in whatever form, is more deadly than earthly pride. It ruins the soul much more quickly than worldly vanity.

D.—And then what is extravagance? That was the second obstacle you spoke of.

F.—Yes. Extravagance is the next obstacle. A true devotee should be free from extravagance in all its forms. His devotion should neither be excessively emotional nor unnecessarily self-torturing. The Gītā says:—

"Yoga is not for him who eats too much, nor for him who eats too little. It is not for him, O Arjuna, who is given to too much sleep, nor for him who keeps vigil too long. But in the case of a man who is temperate in his food and recreation, restrained in all his actions, and regulated in his sleep and vigils, Yoga puts an end to all sorrows."

Again, a true bhakta should avoid extravagance in his attitude to the traditional forms of religion.

D.—What does that mean? What is the correct attitude?

F.—It means that he should neither rest content with the mere external forms of traditional religion, nor go to the other extreme, and set at nought all forms, and claim a dangerous freedom. Nothing kills the spirit of religion so effectively as a mechanical observance of forms through which men's devotions expressed themselves in a bygone age. We should never forget that God endures for ever, but that gods are subject to change and decay. To worship the dead gods is an insult to God. A true bhakta, therefore, should be able to rise above the forms from which the spirit has departed. But, at the same time, he should claim no freedom from the rules and regulations which continue to serve a spiritual purpose. He should not easily bring himself to believe that he is advanced enough to be a law unto himself. He should not set a bad example to his unenlightened fellowmen by setting at nought the forms of established religion. The Gītā says, "Let no enlightened man unsettle the minds of ignorant men who are attached to their work. Himself doing all works with faith, he should make others do as well." If every beginner in religious life tries to discard the letter of the law in the name of the spirit, we shall have chaos in religion. And it is not good for the devotee either. For, very often when the grace of God refuses to come into his consciousness, he has to fall back only on the rests and props of religion, namely, the temple, the offering, the ceremony, the book of devotion, etc.

D.—Father, what do you mean by "the grace of God refusing to come into his consciousness"?

F.—Well, that brings us to the third great obstacle I spoke of—viz., loss of faith. An inexperienced devotee is often tempted to grow impatient when his devotions seem to lead him nowhere, where God hides His head, as it were, and a sense of weariness overwhelms him. Sometimes he has to pass through long stretches of time when religion seems to be a huge self-deception, and the spirit of cynicism makes grimaces at all his attempts at prayer. Sometimes even horrible, unspeakable sins, which normal humanity has outgrown, seem to be perilously near his soul. All the years of illumination, of pious worship and the gracious Presence seem to be rolled away in a moment, and in their place he has only despair and misery. The world, of course, goes on as usual. But to him it is a hard and petrified world with no meaning or purpose. He cannot pray. He cannot meditate. Even the favourite verses of his book of devotion become dull and monotonous with wearisome repetitions. These are the moments which test the strength of a true bhakta.

D.—What should he do then?

F.—He should hold on faithfully to his God amid the gloom. He should never question His will, nor entertain the thought that he did not deserve this treatment. Many a man in this world would be religious, if religion always meant unclouded happiness. Religion *is* unclouded happiness in the end, when the goal is reached. But how many reach the goal before the clouds of mortality have cleared away? An unbroken vision of God in this life is only for a few choice souls, the great founders of the religions of the world, the saviours of our race. But, for the rest of us, when we try to walk in the ways of the Lord, there are many trials, many temptations, much hard work, and many tears, lit up at rare intervals by flashes of a strange light, which is not of this world.

D.—Are these the only obstacles in the way of a devotee?

F.—No. I have indicated to you only the most important and the most obvious of the difficulties in the path of religious life. These and many others are writ large on the lives of some immature bhaktas given in our Purāṇas.

D.—But, father, what about sin? Does it come to an end with the first ascent? Or does it pursue a man even in the second ascent?

F.—My child, in the first ascent, as we have seen, there is a perpetual struggle against sinful acts and sinful thoughts. The way there is full of pitfalls. The pilgrim frequently tumbles down, and frequently rises up. Often he knows where danger lurks, and yet he rushes into the place voluntarily, and, of course, suffers for his folly. It is rather a gloomy path. But when he comes to the second ascent, the sun begins to shine clearly. The pilgrim feels exhilarated. His struggle against sin is now lifted up to a higher plane. He has no longer to fight against the sins of the flesh or the voluntary sins of thought. He is beset only by involuntary sinful thoughts. Like loathsome creatures, they often cross the path of the pilgrim, who simply shudders and passes on, for they do him no more harm.

D.—Father, what are the distinguishing marks of a man who has successfully overcome all these obstacles of the second ascent?

F.—Don't you remember the description of the ideal bhakta given in the twelfth chapter of the Gītā? The Bhagavān says:—

"He who hates none and has kindness and compassion for all, who is free from the feeling of 'I' and 'mine', and who has forbearance, and looks upon pleasure and pain alike;

"He who is ever content and steady in contemplation, who is self-subdued and firm of faith, and who has consecrated his mind and understanding to Me—dear to Me is the man who is thus devoted.

"He from whom the world does not shrink and who does not shrink from the world, and who is free from joy and anger, fear and anxiety—he is dear to Me.

"He who has no wants, who is pure and prompt, unconcerned and untroubled, and who has given up all ambitions—dear to Me is the man thus devoted.

"He who neither rejoices nor hates, neither grieves nor wants and who has renounced both good and evil—dear to Me is the man thus devoted.

"He who is the same to foe and friend and through good and ill repute, who is the same in cold and heat and in pleasure and pain, and who is free from attachments,

"He who is the same in praise and dispraise, who is silent and satisfied with whatever he has, and who is without a home and is firm of mind—dear to Me is the man thus devoted.

"And they who with faith follow this immortal Dharma taught by Me and regard Me as the Supreme—surpassingly dear to Me are they who are thus devoted."

CHAPTER IV

THE THIRD ASCENT

I

D.—To-day I should like to know the state reached by a man who has overcome in this life or in previous lives all the obstacles that lie in the path of religious life described by you the other day.

F.—I have described bhakti as the second ascent in spiritual life. If a man traverses this and reaches the top of the second ascent, it means he is at the foot of the third.

D.—What! Is there another ascent still?

F.—Yes. Have I not already spoken to you of aparā bhakti and parā bhakti? The former leads to the latter. Parā bhakti or jñāna is the third and final ascent in spiritual life. But the difficulty here is the path is not clearly marked, because it is very rarely trodden. And our guides are not agreed. So in what follows we shall first take Śaṁkara as our guide and traverse this difficult ascent, and then we shall take Rāmānuja and then Madhva.

D.—But will you first of all explain to me how the two ascents you have so far described stand in relation to this third ascent?

F.—The moral discipline of the first ascent leads to the mental illumination of the second, which in its turn leads to the spiritual vision of the third. The first is a life of righteousness, the second is a life of devotion, and the third is a life of fulfilment. Just as at the end of the first we saw that morality was not enough, so at the end of the second we see that worship is not the final word in spiritual life. Religious experience, in the narrow sense of the term, is not the highest experience we are capable of. It is indeed true that most of us cannot rise above the level of religious consciousness. But there are exceptional souls who can rise above it to a mystic consciousness. Their experience cannot be ignored. Hinduism faithfully takes into account all types of spiritual experience and correlates them into a graded system. Jñāna is the highest kind of experience which great Ṛṣis acquired after a prolonged life or lives of self-abnegation, prayer and spiritual quest. We therefore cherish it as a priceless possession and regard it as the goal towards which we have to progress.

D.—What is the difference between religious experience and mystic experience?

F.—In all religious experience there is the same implication of duality as in ethical experience. We have seen that in ethical experience there is a perpetual distinction between the ideal and the actual. In religious experience also there is a similar distinction between a perfect God and an imperfect soul. And as long as there is such a distinction, we may take it that the goal is not reached. But in jñāna or mystic experience there is no such distinction. Here, as in God, knowing and being are one. Man knows God by partaking of His nature and becoming divine.

D.—Father, we know the things of the world by means of our intellect. Is jñāna by which we know God different from intellect?

F.—Jñāna is something superior to intellect. It is intuition. It is, as it were, the fulfilment of intellect. Intellect deals with parts and gives therefore only partial or relative truths. Jñāna or Intuition deals with the whole and gives absolute truth. The findings of intuition are not opposed to those of reason. They include them. Intuition does not discard reason, but only supplements it.

D.—Do you mean then that jñāna leads us to a fuller knowledge of God than the intellect?

F.—Yes. There is no comparison between what jñāna reveals and what intellect apprehends. Jñāna is both knowledge of, and life in, God. When our jñāna-cakṣus or the eye of wisdom is opened, we see ourselves as parts and parcels of an abounding divine life, of which the tongue of man can never adequately speak. Our world of time and space then shrinks into a miserably small speck; and we are carried on the waves of a boundless Being, far beyond the little islands of morality and devotion.

II

D.—But, father, I should like to know what exactly this fuller knowledge consists in. What more do we know of God through jñāna in the final stage of spiritual life?

F.—Well, our fuller knowledge consists in knowing how little we really know of Him and how little we *can* know of Him. The feeling that comes over the pilgrim, when he leaves the ascent of bhakti for the higher ascent of jñāna, is not unlike the feeling that came over Arjuna, after he saw the Viśvarūpa or the universal form of Kṛṣṇa described in the Gītā. Arjuna exclaims:—

"If, thinking thou art my friend, not knowing thy greatness, I addressed thee in ignorance or love as 'O Kṛṣṇa, O Yādava, O friend', if in my mirth I showed no reverence to thee while playing or lying down or sitting or eating, alone or in the presence of others, I implore thee to pardon me, infinite and eternal Lord."

In the ascent of bhakti we know only a fragment of Him with reference to ourselves and our childish needs, and like children we affect to be on terms of familiarity with the Father. But on the heights of jñāna our eyes are opened, and we gradually come to see what He is in relation to the universe, and at last what He is in Himself. It is like a child of the royal house growing into a man and coming to know that the father whom he loved and played with hitherto is in truth the great Ruler of an empire, the Lord of life and death, whose will is law to unnumbered nations. Jñāna reveals to us unsuspected heights of grandeur and glory at which we are struck dumb. We come to see that all our boasted knowledge of Him is only ignorance.

D.—Is God then entirely unknowable?

F.—No. It is scientific agnosticism, and not Hinduism, that says that God is unknowable. Agnosticism disclaims all knowledge of spiritual existence, whether God or soul. Agnostics say that behind the physical life of the world there may be God and that behind the mental life of man there may be a soul, but that both of them are unknowable. They say that our knowledge is confined to the field of matter and energy. But Hinduism teaches that God is not only infinitely higher than ourselves but also infinitely near to ourselves. He is nearer to us than our hands and feet. For He is the soul of our souls. He lives in our hearts. He is the canvas on which we shine as painted pictures. He is the very ground of our being.

D.—Then why do you say that the highest wisdom consists in our knowing that we can know very little of Him?

F.—For, though He is present in all of us, we have to cease to be ourselves before we can know Him as He is. We have to learn to transcend time and space. For God lives not only in time, but also beyond time. He is not only immanent, but also transcendent. So how can we, poor creatures of time, form adequate notions of Him who is timeless? Any statement that we may make of Him, any virtue that we may attribute to Him, must fall infinitely short of the reality. After ascribing to Him the highest qualities that we can conceive of, we have to add, "Not simply these but something higher". Therefore the wisest of the Hindu sages declared that the only adequate description of God is "*neti neti*" —not this, not this. Accordingly, in Hinduism we have a twofold conception of God as Saguṇa Brahman or Īśwara, endowed with all the good and glorious qualities that we can think of, raised to the degree of infinity, and Nirguṇa Brahman, the unqualified Godhead which can only be described in negatives. Take, for instance. the following passage from the Gītā:—

"He shines with the faculties of all the senses, and yet He is devoid of senses. He is unattached, and yet He sustains all things. He is without the dispositions of nature, and yet He enjoys them. He is without and within all beings. He has no movement and yet he moves. He is too subtle to be known. He is far away, and yet He is near."

D.—Are not these contradictory conceptions of God?

F.—No, they are complementary conceptions. Suppose you raise your naked eyes to heaven to look at the midday sun. You are dazzled and cannot look at him. Then you use a smoked glass and see him as a red, round globe. The sun you saw at first is not different from the sun you see now. The same sun is blazing in the sky. Similarly, the Absolute in itself is called Brahman. The Absolute in relation to the world, or viewed through human spectacles, is Īśwara. The former is impersonal, the latter is personal.

D.—Then is Īśwara merely a projection of ourselves, and not a reality?

F.—How can you say so? Is the red globe that we see through the smoked glass in place of the sun a projection of ourselves? Īśwara is the best image of Brahman that we can possibly get under our conditions of knowledge. It is the only way in which the Absolute can appear to the human mind.

D.—Then we cannot say that God is both Nirguṇa and Saguṇa. He is Saguṇa to us because of our limitations.

F.—You are right, my child. It is not quite accurate to say that God is both Saguṇa and Nirguṇa. We cannot say that the midday sun is at the same time both blazing and not blazing. It is blazing in itself but not blazing to us when we look through a smoked glass.

D.—You said that the Absolute is impersonal. Do you mean to say that God is not a person?

F.—It all depends upon what we mean by personality. If by personality we mean something finite and limited, then, of course, God is not a person. Usually personality implies the existence of some other being differentiated from the person referred to. Therefore it can belong only to one who stands in some relation to others outside himself. Such a condition cannot obviously apply to God, who is the Absolute, and who is the all. There can be nothing outside God and differentiated from Him. He is not a person standing over against other persons. He is an indivisible Spirit present in all persons. He is the unifying principle behind all creatures. Therefore it is only in an unusual sense that we can use the expression 'personality of God', by which we can only mean the highest conception of God that we, finite beings, can have of Him. To avoid the ambiguity we say that the Absolute in itself is impersonal. The conception of God which the man in the street generally entertains is grossly anthropomorphic.

D.—What does 'anthropomorphic' mean?

F.—'Anthropomorphic' means 'having human form'. The man in the street imagines God as simply a glorified man. As a man eats, enjoys, fights and marries, so does his God eat, enjoy, fight and marry. As a man brings up a family and looks upon his eldest son as his right-hand man in managing his estate, so does his God. As a man pursues and kills his enemy, so does his God. All the ceremonies of popular religion in all countries are designed on this principle. It is repugnance to this rather vulgar religious sentiment that peoples heaven with a host of gods who love and beget that made some of the great minds of the world, like Buddha, silent on the subject of God. Even the God of Gītā, who is tenderly tolerant towards all forms of worship, however imperfect they may be, says, "Fools not knowing My immutable and transcendent nature think that I, the unmanifested, am endowed with a manifest form". But, as men's minds improve, their conception of God becomes elevated and many of the anthropomorphic traits are gradually dropped. By slow degrees God comes to be known as a Being beyond space and time. But even the most cultured of us, for the simple reason that we are men, have to conceive of God, for purposes of religious worship, in terms of personality and interpret our sentiments towards Him in terms of human affections. Else a great spiritual want would be left unsatisfied. At the same time, we owe it to the Supreme Spirit that in our moments of insight we impose on it no such limitations as we are suffering from. We should clearly recognize that God, who is an object of our worship and knowledge, cannot be the Absolute who is above such distinctions as object and subject. We should fearlessly admit that, after all, theism is only a glorified anthropomorphism. That is why our Hindu sages would not stop at this half-way house, but go forward and try to see God as He is, and not simply as He is to us.

D.—Father, if the Absolute should be described only by *neti, neti* —not this, not this—is it not a mere negation or emptiness?

F.—It is not the Absolute that is empty, but our poor human conception of it. All that we mean when we say of the Absolute, that nothing could be predicated of it, is that it is wholly other than what we know in the world. We do not mean that it is a negation or non-being. It is a negation of every positive thing we know. But it is not absolute negation. In other words, we are qualified only to speak of what the Absolute is not, but not of what it is. It is an ineffable Reality, which makes every kind of existence possible in the world. It is like the unseen money in the imperial treasury, which gives the paper currency of a country what value it has. We do not know in what form the money is in the treasury. We have not seen it. But we know that it is there, and it is from the fact of its being there that the currency notes that pass through our hands derive their value. Similarly, we know that the Absolute exists, and that all our moral and spiritual values are derived therefrom. That is why, as the Gītā points out, all our acts of sacrifice, charity and meditation are completed with the formula '*Aum Tat Sat*', which signifies that God is the ultimate Reality from which all our moral and spiritual values are derived.

D.—What is Aum?

F.—The sacred syllable 'Aum' stands in all our religious literature for the Absolute Brahman. The Kaṭha Upaniṣad says:

"The word which all the Vedas proclaim and which all austerities declare, and desiring which men lead a life of chastity—that word I will tell thee briefly. It is Aum. This syllable is indeed Brahman, this syllable is indeed the highest."

And the Māṇḍūkya Upaniṣad, which gives a full exposition of the symbolism of Aum, begins thus:—

"Aum—this syllable is the whole world. Its further explanation is—the past, the present, the future, everything is just the syllable Aum. And whatever else transcends the three-fold time—that too is just the syllable, Aum."

So 'Aum' is the symbol of the Absolute. Hence it is considered the very essence of the Veda.

D.—Father, can we assert nothing about the Absolute represented by Aum except that it exists?

F.—Well, strictly speaking, nothing more can be asserted. For we cannot assert anything without excluding from it what is opposed to it. And the Being from whom something is excluded cannot be called the Absolute. However, we speak of the Absolute as being sat-cit-ānanda.

D.—Father, I have often heard these words repeated. What do they mean?

F.—'Sat' means existence, 'cit' means intelligence, and 'ānanda' means bliss. The whole formula, saccidānanda, simply means that the Absolute exists, it is pure spirit, and it is perfect. In other words, saccidānanda, as applied to Brahman, means that it is a spiritual perfection.

D.—Father, you sometimes speak of God, and sometimes speak of the Absolute. What is the difference?

F.—When we speak of Him as distinct from the world we generally use the term God or Īśwara. But when we speak of Him as including everything, we use the term the Absolute or Brahman.

D.—If the Absolute is perfect bliss how can He contain within Himself this world which is so full of evil and misery? Is He not affected by these? In the first place, why does He allow them to exist?

F.—Evil is inherent in the world. It is a necessary element. For it is the opposition of the finite to the infinite. The infinite is, as it were, imprisoned in the shell of the finite. It has to break the shell, undergo pain and suffering before it comes into its own. Just as a child learns to walk by frequently falling down and crying, we have to attain to perfection by overcoming evil. Thus evil is essential to our moral and spiritual growth. Hence it is a permanent factor in a growing world. It has to exist as long as there is a single finite being to be reclaimed to infinitude. It may be compared to the shadow which an opaque object casts when it is exposed to light. The shadow vanishes when the opaqueness gives place to transparency. Similarly, evil vanishes when the finite becomes infinite.

D.—But a shadow is unreal. Is evil also unreal?

F.—Evil is real to us. But it has no reality in the Divine Being. Śrī Rāmakṛṣṇa once compared God to a serpent, and evil to its poison. What we call poison is no poison to the serpent. It is a normal healthy secretion. The serpent does not die of its own poison. Therefore we say that evil is not ultimately real. Accordingly, Tagore, the greatest Hindu poet of our day, thus writes of pain:—

> "She is the vestal virgin consecrated to the service of the immortal perfection, and when she takes her true place before the altar of the infinite she casts off her dark veil and bares her face to the beholder as a revelation of supreme joy."

Now you will understand why in the Hindu conception of Godhead there are no moral attributes. No evil, no morality. Morality always involves an antithesis. It is what it is in contrast to its opposite. Moral good is called good only when it is in the process of formation. But, when it is fully formed, it ceases to be good owing to the absence of evil. It can only be called the perfect, which we indicate by the word 'ānanda'.

D.—But what is the difficulty in believing that evil is ultimately real?

F.—Don't you see at once that such an assumption would lead to the conception of a finite God? If evil were ultimately real, it could never be destroyed. And a God, who is powerless against evil, is no God. Moreover, if evil were something real, opposed to God and outside of Him, how can we depend upon Him for success in our moral enterprise? What guarantee is there that good would ultimately succeed in the world-struggle?

D.—But does not God fight against evil? Does he not come down in the form of an Avatār when evil becomes excessive?

F.—Yes. But we have to remember the distinction between Brahman and Īśwara. It is the latter that fights against evil, for He is the guardian of eternal Dharma. He is ever at war with evil in the universe which is the theatre of the strife. But, when the opposition between the finite and the infinite ceases, and the Absolute Brahman returns, as it were, into His original wholeness, evil disappears. It is because the fighting Īśwara is only Brahman viewed through human spectacles that we have a guarantee that good will ultimately succeed.

D.—What do you mean by the opposition of the finite and the infinite in the universe?

F.—The finite is matter, the infinite is spirit. Hindu philosophers call the former anātman and the latter ātman. The universe is a battle-field where there is perpetual war between these two. The struggle has so far expressed itself on this earth in the form of minerals, plants, animals and men. From matter to life, from life to consciousness, from consciousness to reason, we see the progressive conquest of ātman over anātman. The whole course of evolution consists in the spirit struggling to come into its own. The struggle is, of course, still going on. Evolution is not yet complete.

D.—What would it be when it is complete?

F.—The final stage would be the rendering of all matter into spirit. It is the return of the Absolute into itself. But that is only an ideal like the original separation of the Absolute into matter and spirit.

D.—What? Is it the Absolute itself that became originally separated into matter and spirit?

F.—Yes. The Absolute appears in the universe as the inseparable two—matter and spirit, object and subject, anātman and ātman. These imply each other. They are the sundered parts of an original whole. And the history of the universe is simply a process of the sundered parts getting back to the original wholeness. Therefore true progress is always to be measured by the supremacy of spirit over matter.

III

D.—Father, you say that the Absolute sunders itself and appears as subject and object, or spirit and matter, and that in the end these coalesce and again become the Absolute. Why does the Absolute do this?

F.—My child, who can tell? We may as well ask ourselves, "Why does fire give out heat and light?" It is the nature of the Absolute to manifest itself in the world as the inseparable two, just as it is the nature of fire to give out heat and light.

D.—Is there no motive then for the creation of the world?

F.—What motive can we ascribe to God without impairing His perfection? He has nothing to attain which He has not already attained. He has nothing to desire which He does not already possess. We can therefore only say that it is His līlā or pleasure to manifest Himself in the world, as it is an artist's pleasure to manifest himself in a work of art. But, from our point of view, we may say that by this process He creates opportunities for souls to work out their destinies.

D.—Father, if the world is a manifestation of God, can we not say that the world is God?

F.—No. We cannot say that the world is God, any more than that the Rāmāyaṇa is Vālmīki. No doubt, God is immanent in the world. But His immanence does not mean that He is to be identified with the world. It is Pantheism, and not Hinduism, that identifies God with the universe.

D.—What is Pantheism?

F.—Pantheism is a philosophic theory that assumes that this universe of ours is an exhaustive manifestation of God. It is a half-truth like Deism, another philosophic theory, that assumes that the Creator is entirely outside His creation. Pantheism emphasizes the immanence of God to the exclusion of His transcendence, while Deism emphasizes the transcendence of God to the exclusion of His immanence. Hinduism is neither Pantheism nor Deism. According to it, God is both transcendent and immanent. He is in the world and also beyond it. He is its material cause as well as its efficient cause. He is the clay as well as the potter. Hence Hindu scriptures compare the world to a spider's web, the threads of which come out of the spider itself. But the web is not the spider. Similarly, the world is not God. The finite manifests the infinite, but it does not manifest the whole of the infinite. The God of the Gītā says that the whole universe is sustained by a *part* of Himself, and that it lives in Him, and not He in it. Also, while admitting that all things are divine, Hinduism recognizes that some things reveal God more than others. A plant is more divine than a mineral, an animal is more divine than a plant, a man is more divine than an animal, and a good man is more divine than a bad man. Thus from the lowest atom of dust to the highest Īśwara all are in God, but all are not equally divine.

D.—So does the existence of the world mean that at one time a small fraction of the infinite became finite?

F.—We cannot say that. For the relation of whole and part does not apply to the Absolute who is the All. When we speak of God as the whole, and the world as the part we only use a figurative language which is not strictly true.

D.—Do you mean to say, then, that neither the whole of the Absolute nor a part of the Absolute has become the world?

F.—Yes. For if we say it is the whole, then the Absolute becomes the world, and all our search for God beyond this finite world becomes futile. If we say it is a part, then we apply to the Absolute the relation of whole and part which is inapplicable to it.

D.—How then do you explain the origin of the world?

F.—Well, we cannot exactly explain how this changing, finite world of ours came into existence, nor how it is connected with the unchanging, infinite God. The Gītā, speaking of the world-tree, says:—

"Its form is not here perceived as such, neither its end, nor its origin, nor its existence."

Various theories of creation have been put forward by different schools of Indian thought.

D.—What are they?

F.—The most important of them are—āraṁbha-vāda, pariṇāma-vāda and vivarta-vāda.

D.—What is āraṁbha-vāda?

F.—The theory of the Nyāya-Vaiśeṣika school of philosophers is known as āraṁbha-vāda. According to this, at the beginning of a kalpa invisible and intangible atoms of different orders, under the influence of the will of God and the destiny of souls, unite to form the various objects of the world, differing in their qualities from the atoms themselves. Thus the effect is entirely different from the cause. It comes into being anew, as a cloth comes into being anew when the threads are put together. The atoms combine with one another and continue in combination giving rise to the various objects of the world for some time, and then they separate, so that the whole effect collapses. This process of creation and destruction goes on till the time of mahāpralaya or final dissolution. Such is their theory.

D.—What is Pariṇāma-vāda?

F.—The theory of the Sāṁkhya school is known as pariṇāma-vāda. It is a theory of evolution. According to this, the universe consists of two eternal realities, one conscious and the other unconscious. The former is called Puruṣa and the latter Pradhāna. There is an infinite number of Puruṣas all independent of one another and devoid of any qualities. They are the silent spectators of the various modifications of Pradhāna.

D.—What is Pradhāna?

F.—The Pradhāna, otherwise called Prakṛti, of the Sāṁkhya system is either universal matter or universal energy. It has three **guṇas** or dispositions, namely, sattva or goodness, rajas or passion and tamas or dullness. When these three are in equilibrium, Pradhāna is quiescent. When this equilibrium is disturbed by the presence of souls, the guṇas act on one another and we have evolution. And this gives rise to the following:—mahat or buddhi which means cosmic intellect; ahaṁkāra or self-consciousness; the five so-called tanmātras of sound, touch, smell, form and taste; the means or mind; the five organs of cognition; the five organs of action; and finally the five gross elements of ether, air, light, water and the earth. The evolving Prakṛti is in itself blind and unconscious, but all its activities are purposive, the purpose being the fulfilment of what is conceived as the destiny of souls. At the end of a kalpa or world-period the world is dissolved, and the three guṇas of Pradhāna come into equilibrium again. The Sāṁkhya theory is an improvement on that of the Nyāya-Vaiśeṣika. For it postulates only two ultimate realities, while the latter postulates a number of ultimate realities. The Vaiśeṣika system, by the way, is in itself an improvement on Buddhistic nihilism, which declares that nothing is real or permanent. Again, while according to the Nyāya theory, as we have seen, the effect is different from the cause, according to the Sāṁkhya theory the effect is inherent in the cause. It is only made manifest by evolution, as oil is made manifest when the oil-seed is pressed.

D.—And what is vivarta-vāda?

F.—This is a theory of appearance and reality. According to some schools of Vedānta, the cause without undergoing any change in itself, produces the effect. Threads have to be woven together to produce a cloth. Oil seeds have to be pressed together for oil to come out. In both these cases the cause undergoes a change. So these analogies will not do to explain creation in which the Creator remains unaffected by the process. Therefore some philosophers use the well-known figures of a rope appearing as a snake in the dark, a pillar as a ghost, a piece of shell as silver, and a sandy desert as a mirage. The rope, the pillar, the shell, and the desert are realities, while the snake, the ghost, the silver and the mirage are only appearances. The different illustrations used are intended to indicate the dependence of the effect upon the cause, and, at the same time, the changelessness of the cause. What is really God appears to our finite intelligence as the universe of time and space, just as a piece of rope appears in the twilight as a snake, or a pillar appears in the dark as a ghost. When we come to feel that it is only a rope or a pillar, we no longer fear it, we no longer run away from it. Similarly, when we come to realize God, we are no longer troubled by the appearances of the world. When Avidyā or the veil of misapprehension is removed by Vidyā or divine knowledge, when mithyā-jñāna or false knowledge is replaced by Saṁyakdarśana or true perception, we rise to a higher order of reality, as a dreamer rises into waking life. This is a matter of spiritual experience, and all the mystics of the world have borne testimony to it. But how exactly the Reality is connected with the appearance we are not able to see in the present state of our knowledge. The relation is therefore said to be anirvacanīya or indefinable. God, by His Māyā, brings about this wonderful phenomenon of creation.

D.—What does Māyā mean? Does it is not mean illusion? If so, is this world unreal?

F.—It was some Buddhist philosophers who preached that the world was unreal. Their opinions were condemned as heretical. No orthodox Vedic school ever supported the theory of illusionism, according to which nothing really exists outside our minds. On the other hand, we distinguish three stages in Hindu philosophy in the treatment of this question of the reality of the world. The first stage of development is seen in the theories of Nyāya-Vaiśeṣika which analyzed the facts of the world and reduced them, as we have already seen, into a number of padārthas or categories. The second stage of development is seen in the theories of Sāṁkhya-Yoga, which further reduced them to the two well-known categories of Prakrti and Puruṣa. The third stage of development is seen in the theories of the various schools of Vedānta which tackle the question whether it is not possible to reduce the two to one. The systems of Rāmānuja, Madhva, Nimbārka and Vallabha teach that the world is real, but dependent on God in one way or another. Thus one of the two categories is made subordinate to the other. Śaṁkara goes a step further. He does not deny the reality of the world, as he is often supposed to do. Far from teaching such a doctrine, he takes pains to refute the Buddhist theory of illusionism. According to him, the world is real as you and I are real. A subject implies an object, and an object implies a subject. Each depends upon the other. If the perceiving subject were entirely independent of the objective world, he would move in a phantom world of his own creation. And if the objective world were entirely independent of any perceiving subject, it would be a chaotic world of dark forces and vibrations, and not a world of light and colour, or of law and order. The former view leads to a fanciful idealism, and the latter to a crude realism. The world is emphatically not an illusion. It exists in its own right, as the human mind exists in its own right. As long as the mind is real, the world also is real. But both belong to a lower order of reality than the Absolute. They are only relatively real, while God is absolutely real. Let me take an illustration. Have you read Kālidāsa's Śākuntalam?

D.—Yes, father. I have read a Telugu translation.

F.—Well, any drama will suit my purpose. In Kālidāsa's play, in the first act, we see that King Duṣyanta enters the hermitage of Kaṇva and sees Śakuntalā and her companions watering the plants. Does the king look upon the hermitage as illusion? Does he treat Śakuntalā and her companions or himself as phantoms?

D.—No, of course not.

F.—But are not the characters really the phantoms of the poet's brain? Is not the hermitage of Kaṇva a sweet dream of Kālidāsa's? You see there are two orders of reality here—Duṣyanta and his fellow characters on the one hand, and Kālidāsa and his readers on the other. Within the limits of the drama everything is real—plot, situation and characterization. But the dramatist belongs to a higher order of reality. From his standpoint, the characters are only ideal creations. Similarly, from the standpoint of God, we and the world in which we live are unreal. But among ourselves and relatively to one another we are terribly real. The world is there external to our minds. But there is nothing external to the mind of God.

D.—But do not our scriptures sometimes describe the world as a dream?

F.—Yes. But to whom is the world a dream? Not certainly

to the man of the world. A dream is no dream to the dreamer. It is a terrible reality to him. It is only to the awakened man that it is a dream. Similarly, it is not to the man of the world, but to the Yogin in his samādhi, when he identifies himself with the changeless Reality, that the world seems unreal. We are all of us in a world which is real to us; but we aspire to the attainment of a world, which the Veda reveals to us, and in which this will o' the wisp of a world, with its deceits and lies, its cruel mockeries and temptations, will not bewilder us any further.

D.—You say then that Māyā is not merely illusion, as it is generally understood?

F.—Yes. That is what I have tried to say.

D.—Then what is Māyā?

F.—Māyā is strictly speaking, a mystery. It is the indefinable power by which God, while remaining Himself changeless, appears as the changing universe. That is why we sometimes say that Māyā is the cause of the world, and that it is the same as Prakṛti. And as it is only to finite beings like ourselves that God so appears, our finiteness is also called Māyā. Thus Māyā is both subjective and objective. The subjective aspect is also called Avidyā.

D.—What exactly is Avidyā?

F.—Avidyā is the natural disability of the soul which prevents it from apprehending God as He really is. Man as man can never know God. He should transcend his upādhis and become divine to know the Divine Being.

IV

D.—What are upādhis?

F.—Upādhis are the limitations of our souls. They are simply the physical, mental and moral conditions under which we have to work in life. Their exact analysis is a matter of science, and may change from time to time. The ancient psychologists of India analyzed them thus. There is, first of all, the gross body which is made up of various elements and which the soul casts off at death. But destruction of the physical body does not bring freedom to the soul. For even after death, it is still enclosed by a subtle body, with which are associated the subtle organs of perception and action, the mind, and the vital breath. The soul wanders through the mazes of saṁsāra always with this psychic equipment, its course being determined by the merit of its deeds. Till the upādhiṣ, which are imposed on it by Avidyā, are transcended by means of Vidyā or spiritual insight, each soul imagines that it is separate from other souls and separate from God. Man deludes himself into the belief that he is an independent unit. Hence he is subject to birth and death.

D.—Are not souls really separate from one another?

F.—Souls are as separate from one another as the islands in the ocean, or the leaves on a tree. The islands in the ocean appear as separate places with different physical features and different vegetable and mineral products. But we know that deep down in the ocean they are all connected together by land. Without that internal connection they can never stand. So also individual souls. For all practical purposes the individual is a separate unit. He is a moral agent. He sins and falls. He does good, and is raised As he sows, he reaps in this world or in the next. But his salvation lies in his finally transcending his individuality. At first sight we may all seem to be rigidly apart from one another. But a moment's consideration will show that we understand one another, love one another and enter into one another's mind. This sense of unity, raised to its maximum, constitutes the mystic vision of the living unity of all creation. Thus what we deny is not the existence of the individual soul, but its ultimate reality as a separate and independent unit. When the limitations of body, mind and understanding are removed the individual is no longer an individual, he becomes one with the infinite Spirit, just as when a closed jar or pot is broken the space hitherto enclosed becomes one with the infinite space. Accordingly, as on the question of the reality of the world, we have here also a higher view and a lower view. The lower view, namely, that there are separate individual souls, is not a false view. It is only a partial view. It gives one aspect of the truth, not the whole truth. Error comes in only when we mistake what is relatively real for what is absolutely real.

D.—Is it also an error to think that our souls are separate from God? You said that was also a part of Avidyā?

F.—Yes. Every individual soul is only a focus, as it were, in one infinite consciousness. Or, it is a point in the universe where the veil of time and space is so thin that we see the infinite Spirit behind.

D.—Is the soul then a part of God?

F.—No. For, as we have seen, the conception of part and whole does not apply to God.

D.—It is then a form or modification of God.

F.—No. For, God cannot really be subject to any change or modification.

D.—What then is its relation to God?

F.—When the upādhis are removed, what we call the individual soul is seen to be identical with the universal soul.

D.—Is that the logical conclusion?

F.—It is not a mere logical conclusion. It is the highest teaching of the Veda. The ultimate identity of the soul and God—of the individual soul and the universal soul—is established by four mahāvākyas or great utterances taken from the four Vedas.

D.—What are these mahāvākyas?

F.—The Aitareya Upaniṣad of the Ṛg-Veda says, "Prajñānam Brahma" or "Intelligence is Brahman". The Bṛhadāraṇyaka Upaniṣad of the Yajur-Veda says, "Aham Brahmāsmi" or "I am Brahman". The Chāndogya Upaniṣad of the Sāma-Veda says, "Tattvamasi" or "Thou art That". And lastly the Atharva-Veda says, "Ayam Ātmā Brahma" or "This self is Brahman".

D.—Father, the soul is confined to the body, and is subject to pains and sorrows. How can it be identical with the infinite Spirit which is all bliss?

F.—It is a mistake to suppose that the soul is in the body. On the other hand it is truer to say that the body is in the soul. The body is enveloped and pervaded by the soul which is infinite, all-pervading and eternal. The body is like a vessel, and the soul is like the space within it and without it. When the vessel is moved from place to place, the space within it is not moved. When the contents of the vessel are boiled, the space or ether in it is not boiled. Similarly, there is in us something uncreated, something untouched by sin or suffering. The Gītā, quoting from the Kaṭhopaniṣad, says, "It is said that the senses are great, but greater than the senses is the mind, and greater than the mind is the understanding, but what is even greater than the understanding is He."

D.—The soul is subject to birth and death while the eternal Spirit is not. How can both be identical?

F.—Birth is only the union of the soul with the body, and death the separation from it. The soul in itself is eternal. It is not born, nor does it die.

D.—What happens to the soul after it is separated from the body? Does it become one with the universal Soul?

F.—It cannot become one with the universal Soul till all its upādhis are removed. And I have already said that death removes only one of the upādhis, namely, the gross body. But there is still the subtle body, and there is the acquired merit or demerit which determines its next birth.

D.—When are these also removed?

F.—They are removed only when the soul qualifies itself for mokṣa or salvation.

D.—You say that the soul is ultimately identical with God. What new qualifications has it to acquire?

F.—The soul *is* identical with God. But it is subject to upādhis on account of its Avidyā. These prevent it from realizing its identity. The soul need not, strictly speaking, acquire new qualifications. It has only to remove its disqualifications. For salvation, being of the nature of eternity, is not something that is made, but something that is only realized.

D.—How is this Avidyā removed?

F.—It is removed by Vidyā or Jñāna. Avidyā, as we have seen, consists in our imagining that we are separate from one another and separate from God. All our sin and suffering are due to this ajñāna or false notion. The individual soul has to learn to transcend its individuality.

D.—How is this done?

F.—By righteousness, by love and by spiritual insight a man has to go out of himself and feel the oneness of all beings in God. This feeling should become an abiding possession. Then the scales fall from his eyes, the vision of God comes to him, and he realizes the truth of the mahāvākyas of the Śruti.

D.—Is it not enough if he constantly meditates on the identity taught by the mahāvākyas?

F.—Can an exiled king get back his kingship by shutting his eyes and thinking "I am the king, I am the king"? No. He should marshall his scattered forces, win over allies and conquer his enemies, and come into his own. Similarly, we should subdue our selfishness, conquer our passions, love the God that is within us and realize that He is present in all creatures. **In fact, we should traverse the three ascents of work, worship** and wisdom that I have been describing to you in these talks.

The Saṁyakdarśana or the true and full vision, which gives us mokṣa, is to be had only on the summit of the third ascent.

D.—When a man does not live to reach the summit, but dies on the way either in the first or the second ascent, what happens to his soul? Is all his effort lost? And does he perish?

F.—In reply to a similar question put by Arjuna to Kṛṣṇa in the Gītā, the latter says, "Neither in this world nor in the next, O Arjuna, would he perish. For a man who does good, my dear, will never come to grief."

D.—But what happens to him?

F.—Our scriptures describe two paths for the dead—the Pitṛyāna and the Devayāna. Those who fall and die in the first ascent which I described have to come back into the world of time and change. They take birth in surroundings suitable to their further progress. In other words, their past karma, good and bad, determines for them their environment such as country, nation, class, parentage, etc. This path is the Pitṛyāna. Those who fall and die while scaling the second ascent never come back into the time-process. They never take birth again.

D.—Do they obtain mokṣa?

F.—No. They are not yet qualified for mokṣa, for mokṣa comes only after the Saṁyakdarśana of the third ascent. But their further progress is ensured in a world of Spirit which is called Brahma-loka. There they live with more than human faculties in the presence of the God whom they worshipped on earth. And finally they attain mukti. This path is the Devayāna; and, as the mukti reached along this path is gradual, it is called kramamukti.

D.—Why is there such a difference between the fate of those who fall in the first ascent and that of those who fall in the second ascent? Why do the former come back into this dark world of ours and the latter go to the bright world of Brahma-loka?

F.—It is because works, however virtuous they may be, do not involve a total effacement of the self. Morality exalts and purifies an individual, but he still remains an individual. His virtues and vices have a hold over him. But, as we have seen, the very essence of mokṣa consists in an individual breaking down the walls of his isolation. Therefore a man, who dies before this is done, has naturally to return to this world of space and time, that is, of individuality and exclusion. But in the religious worship of the second ascent the individual takes refuge in the object of his worship and totally forgets himself. Therefore his virtues and vices have no hold over him. He is in the hands of God whose grace leads him into a higher world and prepares him for mokṣa. Hence his path is different from that of the man who dies in the first stage.

D.—What is the state of the soul after it attains mokṣa?

F.—I have already said that mokṣa means the awakening of the soul into divine life and coming into its own. So the state of such a soul is the same as that of the Divine Being. Let me quote two passages from the Veda which describe that state:—

"He who verily knows the supreme Brahman becomes Brahman."

"As the flowing rivers in the ocean
Disappear, quitting name and form,
So the knower, being liberated from name and form,
Goes unto the heavenly Person, higher than the high."

There are, of course, differences of opinion among teachers of the Vedānta about the correct interpretation of these passages, as about almost all the subjects we have been discussing to-day. We are following Śaṁkara now, and presently we shall come back to the views of the other teachers.

D.—Father, can a man attain moksa while remaining in this body?

F.—There is nothing to prevent it, my child. Such a person is called Jīvanmukta. By the Saṁyakdarśana that he obtains on the summit of the third ascent, the effects of his former karma are all destroyed except the small fraction of prārabdha karma which has come to fruition in the present body. He remains in the body till the effect of this are over. As his present actions are the outcome, not of his selfish desire, but of his union with God, they bear no seeds of future lives; and as his present devotions are the outcome, not of any great gulf between him and God, but of an enlightened self-knowledge, they need no further life of probation. So a Jīvanmukta acts in the world and worships God, but he is absolutely free. That is the teaching of the Śruti and the Śmṛti. Śaṁkara, in a famous passage in his Sūtra-Bhāṣya, gives us a hint of his own personal experience in this matter. He says, "It is not a matter for dispute at all whether the body of a Brahmavit, or one who has realized Brahman, continued to exist for some time or not. For how can man contest another's heartfelt conviction that he has realized Brahman although he continues to have a bodily existence?"

D.—Father, what is the sort of life that a Jīvanmukta leads?

F.—How can I describe it in a few words? The whole of the Bhagavad-Gītā may be looked upon as an exposition of this character. For a Jīvanmukta is a perfect Yogin. He possesses, on the one hand, an unclouded experience of the absolute reality of Brahman and of the identity of his own self with it, and, on the other, the consciousness of the relative character of all that is different from it, namely, the world, his own body and the other upādhis of the soul. He has, of course, neither pains nor sorrows, neither fears nor desires. He is far above the pitiful pleasures of this world. Sin can never approach him and he has no need to make an effort to be virtuous. He has no need of prayers either. For he feels the holy presence of God in him constantly, and life is no mystery to him. Scriptures are superfluous to him, for they have all fulfilled their object. The Veda itself says of such a man, "To him the Veda is no Veda". So he becomes a real Svarāt or one who has attained to the perfect spiritual freedom of God. His soul lives on the heights of divine peace and joy. But he voluntarily works in the world as God works, not for any object of his own, but for the good of others. He takes part in the human drama, not to please himself or the other actors, but the divine stage-manager whose interests are his own. Even after he quits this body he gladly takes up another, if his presence is required in the world. Such is the life of a Jīvanmukta. All the great saints of the world and the founders of religions that have profoundly influenced the history of humanity are, more or less, Jīvanmuktas. The aim of all our studies, of all our mental and moral disciplines and of all our spiritual endeavours is only to develop in course of time this type of character.

V

D.—Father, you said there were differences of opinion among Hindu teachers about the third ascent. May I know what they are?

F.—There are three important schools of Vedānta—the Advaita of Śaṃkara, the Viśiṣṭādvaita of Rāmānuja and the Dvaita of Madhva.

D.—How do these differ from one another?

F.—There are considerable differences with regard to the four chief topics we discussed to-day, namely, God and His creation, and the soul and its salvation. The view that I have so far given is that of Śaṃkara's Advaita. I will now give you a short account of Rāmānuja's Viśiṣṭādvaita, from which you will see how his teaching differs from Śaṁkara's.

According to Rāmānuja, the Absolute is not impersonal, but a personality endowed with all the glorious qualities we know of, such as knowledge, power and love. So God is saguṇa only, and not nirguṇa. The Vedic texts, which deny qualities to Him, should be interpreted as meaning that He has no such lower qualities as sorrow, change, mortality, etc. The difference that is necessary for the idea of the personality of God exists in Himself. For He has two inseparable prakāras or modes, namely, the world and souls. These are related to Him, as the body is related to the soul. They inhere in him as attributes in a substance. But they have two phases—the subtle phase and the manifest phase, according as God is in His kāraṇa-avasthā, *i.e.*, causal state, or kārya-avasthā, *i.e.*, effected state. The former is the state before creation, and the latter after creation.

Creation is an act of God by which souls and matter undergo transformations. Matter is fundamentally real and it undergoes a real pariṇāma or evolution, and not simply an apparent variation. Even after pralaya or dissolution matter exists, as in the beginning, in a subtle state as the prakāra of

God. Therefore it is eternal, though very dependent.

The soul is a higher prakāra of God than matter, because it is a conscious entity. It is also eternally real and eternally distinct from God and eternally dependent on Him. It is as uncreated as matter, creation only meaning in this case the expansion of intelligence and the acquisition of a material body according to the degree of merit acquired in a previous existence. Moreover the soul is ever atomic (aṇu) in size dwelling in the heart like a point of light and therefore distinct from God who is all-pervasive (vibhu). There are three classes of souls—nitya, mukta and baddha. To the first class belong those who are eternally free and who live with God in Vaikuṇṭha, His supreme abode. To the second class belong those who were once subject to saṁsāra but who have now acquired salvation and live with God. And to the third class belong those who are still in the meshes of saṁsāra and who are striving to be saved.

Salvation can be obtained only by the grace of God, responding to the call of bhakti and prapatti or self-surrender on the part of the worshipper. Karma and jñāna are only means to bhakti. The released souls attain to the nature of God and never to identity with him. They remain atomic in size and dependent in their nature on God. They live in fellowship with Him either serving Him or meditating on Him. Thus they never lose their individuality, they are only released from saṁsāra. And this release comes only after quitting the body, for, according to Rāmānuja there is no such thing as Jīvanmukti.

D.—Father, will you please let me know the specific points of difference between Śaṁkara's system and Rāmānuja's system?

F.—From the brief account of the Viśiṣṭādvaita that I have just now given, you will see that it differs from the Advaita in the following points:—

1. To Rāmānuja God is always personal endowed with various perfections. But to Śaṁkara God is both personal and supra-personal. In relation to the world He is conceived as being endowed with various perfections, but in Himself He is really different from anything we can conceive of.

2. To Rāmānuja the world is absolutely real being an inseparable prakāra or mode of God. But to Śaṁkara the world is only relatively real. It is real to the individual soul only so long as its individuality lasts.

3. To Rāmānuja the jīva or individual soul is also absolutely real and eternally distinct from God, though God, being omnipresent, dwells in it. But to Śaṁkara, on the other hand, the jīva is only relatively real, its individuality lasting only so long as it is subject to upādhis or limiting conditions.

4. To Rāmānuja mokṣa is freedom from saṁsara But to Śaṁkara it is freedom from not only saṃsāra but also freedom from exclusive individuality and its corollary, the conception of a phenomenal world.

5. To Rāmānuja karma and jñāna are only means to bhakti which gives mokṣa. But to Śaṃkara karma and bhakti are means to jñāna which *is* mokṣa.

D.—And how does the Dvaita differ from these?

F.—The Dvaita philosophy of Madhva has many points in common with the Viśiṣṭādvaita of Rāmānuja. To Madhva, as to Rāmānuja, there are three eternal entities fundamentally different from one another—God, the soul and the world. Of these God is a svatantra or an independent reality, and the other two are paratantras or dependent realities. He does not create them, but only rules them. To Madhva, as to Rāmānuja, God is a person whose grace is necessary for the salvation of the devotee. Like Rāmānuja, Madhva identifies God with Viṣṇu living in Vaikuṇṭha along with His consort Lakṣmī, who is the personification of His creative power. God manifests himself through various vyūhas or forms and avatārs or incarnations. He is also the antaryāmin or the inner controller of all souls. And, lastly, to Madhva, as to Rāmānuja, souls are of atomic size and are of three kinds—nitya, mukta and baddha. These are the points of agreement.

D.—But what are the points of difference?

F.—Madhva differs from Rāmānuja in the following points:—

1. Madhva does not admit that the world is the body of God. According to him God is only the efficient cause of the world, and not the material cause. The distinction between God and the world of matter and souls is absolute and unqualified. That is why his system is called Dvaita or dualism, while Śaṁkara's system which denies any such ultimate distinction is called Advaita or monism; and Rāmānuja's system, which maintains the distinction but also emphasizes the oneness of the Absolute, is called Viśiṣṭādvaita or qualified monism.

2. Madhva holds that, though every atom of space in the universe is filled with jīvas, no two jīvas are alike in character. They are essentially different from one another and belong to different grades even in their enjoyment of bliss after salvation.

3. Madhva further classifies the souls that are still bound to the wheel of saṁsāra into three classes—(i) those who, being of sāttvika

nature, are pre-ordained for salvation; (ii) those who, being of rajasa nature, are pre-ordained to wander for all time in the labyrinth of saṁsāra; (iii) those who being of tamasa nature, are pre-ordained to suffer in eternal darkness.

4. Madhva holds that souls cannot get salvation except through a mediator who gives them the saving knowledge. This mediator is Vāyu, the son of Viṣṇu.

But, my child, these are rather subtle differences which are bound to arise in the bosom of a religion which is singularly free from rigid dogmas and which encourages rather than discourages freedom of opinion. They are of little practical importance. They do not stand in the way of men perfecting their lives through righteousness, love and worship in accordance with the main teaching of our scriptures. It is therefore enough for you to confine yourself to matters on which all our teachers are agreed.

D.—Will you kindly tell me what the points are on which all are agreed?

F.—All Hindu religious teachers are agreed in thinking:—

1. **That the spiritual experience embodied in the Śruti is our ultimate authority in religion, and not mere individual reason;**

2. **That God is One though He has many names and forms, and that He is an ineffable perfection;**

3. **That all men find themselves in this life in the toils of samsara in accordance with their own past karma;**

4. **That there is a triple path consisting of karma, bhakti and jñāna which can lead men out of saṁsara to the perfection of God;**

5. **That he who would be saved should cultivate the virtues of purity, self-control, detachment, truth and ahiṁsā in their various forms and become a Dharmātmā;**

6. **That he has further to worship his Iṣṭa-Devatā according to his adhikāra, and, by every means in his power, acquire the grace of God;**

7. **That his salvation consists in his being free from the cycle of births and deaths and gaining entrance into the world of Spirit.**

These are the things that really matter. They are the teachings that fill our lives with hope, and give a meaning and content to all our struggles here against ignorance and sin.

VI

D.—Father, have you done?

F.—Yes, my child, I have. I hope the account I have given you of the three ascents of the path of light will enable you to lead a complete spiritual life of virtue, devotion and insight. It is only for purposes of instruction that I have made the three ascents separate from one another. In truth, long before you reach the top of the first ascent you are on the second, and long before you reach the top of the second you are on the third. Spiritual life is one. It is made up of the three elements of karma, bhakti and jñāna that vary in their proportions according to the temperament of the striving soul.

Now my task is over. I have given you a short account of the essentials of a religion which, though it is the oldest in the world, is as vigorous to-day as any other religion, and which is professed by 230 millions of men—a considerable part of the human race. Incidentally, I have also pointed out that Hinduism is neither fatalism nor pessimism, neither asceticism nor quietism, neither agnosticism nor pantheism, neither illusionism nor mere polytheism, as some of its hasty critics have represented it to be. It is a synthesis of all types of religious experience, from the highest to the lowest. It is a whole and complete view of life. That is why it has stood like a rock all these thousands of years and survived the attacks of the followers of all the other great religions of the world. It has survived the Buddhist schism of ancient times, the Muslim oppression of mediaevel times, and the Christian propaganda of modern times. And to-day in the twentieth century, it is again in one of its Periods of Renaissance. It looks ahead and sees a glorious future before it. No wonder, therefore, that the Hindus call their religion Sanātana Dharma or eternal order, and are justly proud of it. Dull must he be of soul indeed whose pulse does not throb when he reads the history of Hindu Civilization extending over more than forty centuries, and takes into account its achievements in social organization as well as literature and art. No doubt this civilization has had its reverses. It has its sins—many grievous sins—to answer for. Which civilization has not? Let us frankly admit every one of them, and try to put our house in order. Let us march on and make our future worthy of our past. It is with this hope that I have endeavoured to show to you, and through you to the youth of India, the steel frame that lies behind all the bewildering castes and sects of Hinduism.

I hope also that your own life will fulfil the promise that it is holding out now, and make you worthy of the sacred name you bear.

D.—As God wills!

F.—Yes, my dear. As God wills! There is no religion higher than that.

APPENDIX

Scriptural Selections

We are giving below some selections from the two most important Hindu scriptures—the Upanishads and the Bhagavad Gita. They are arranged under three heads—God, Soul and Spiritual Practice. In spite of this arrangement, many of them will be found to overlap in part or even in the whole of their meaning. So also the Personal and the Impersonal conceptions of the Deity, His transcendent and immanent aspects, may be mixed up in the same passage. The line of demarcation between the Soul (the individual spirit) and God (the universal spirit) is often very thin and sometimes almost non-existent. This mixing up in the selections cannot be avoided, because it is a characteristic feature of the texts themselves. It is hoped that the selective reading of these texts will be found helpful by the students.

GOD

That which cannot be comprehended by the mind but by which the mind is cognized know that alone to be Brahman, and not this that people worship here. **(Kena I.6)**

The wise man relinquishes both joy and sorrow having realized, by means of meditation on the inner Self, that ancient effulgent One, hard to be seen, subtle, immanent, seated in the heart and residing within the body. **(Katha I.2.12)**

The goal which all Vedas proclaim, which all penances declare, and desiring which they lead the life of Brahmacharya,—I tell it to thee in brief—it is Om. This syllable is Brahman; this syllable is also the highest. Having known this syllable, whatever one desires one gets that. **(Ibid. I.2.15,16)**

Whatever is here, that is there; what is there, the same is here. He who sees here as different meets with death again and again. By mind alone is It to be realized and (then,) there is no difference here. From death to death he goes, who sees as if there is difference here. **(Ibid. II.1.10,11)**

He is the sun dwelling in the heavens, the air dwelling in the sky, the fire existing on the altar, the guest (Soma) dwelling in the jar; He is in man, in the gods, in the sacrifice, in the sky; (He is) born in water, born on earth, born in the sacrifice, born on the mountains; (He is) the true; (He is) the great. **(Ibid. II.2.2)**

The Purusha who remains awake shaping (all sorts of) objects of desires even while we sleep,—verily that is the pure, the Brahman, and that is also called the immortal. In that rest all the worlds, and none can transcend that. This verily is that. **(Ibid. II.2.8)**

The sun does not shine there, nor the moon and the stars, nor these lightnings, and much less this fire. When that shines, every thing shines after that. By its light all this is lighted. **(Ibid. II.2.15)**

This is the ancient Asvattha tree whose roots are above and whose branches (spread) below. That is verily the pure, that is Brahman, and that is also called the immortal. In that rest all the worlds, and none can transcend it. Verily this is that. **(Ibid. II.3.1)**

(Brahman is seen) in the self as (one sees oneself) in the mirror; in the world of manes, as (one perceives oneself) in dream; in the world of Gandharvas, as (one's reflection) is seen in the water; in the world of Brahma, as light and shade. **(Ibid. II.3.5)**

Beyond the senses is the mind, beyond the mind is the intellect, beyond the intellect is the Great Atman. Superior to the Great Atman is the Unmanifested. And verily beyond also the Unmanifested is the all-pervading Purusha devoid of all distinctive marks, knowing whom (every) creature is emancipated and attains immortality. His form is not within the field of vision. None can see Him with the eyes. He is revealed by the intuition of the intellect which resides in the heart and controls the mind. Those who know Him become immortal. **(Ibid. II.3.7–9)**

What is invisible, ungraspable, unoriginated and attributeless; what has neither eyes, nor ears, nor hands, nor feet; what is eternal, all-pervading immeasurably subtle and limitless in manifestation;—that Imperishable Being is what the wise perceive as the source of all creation. As the spider emits and withdraws the web, as herbs sprout on the earth, as hair grows on the head and body of man without any effort,—so from the Imperishable Being the universe springs out. From brooding thought Brahman swells (with the joy of creation). Thence food is born and from it energy, mind, the true, the worlds, and endless entanglements in works. Brahma the Creator, individual beings, and nourishment for creatures—these spring from Him, the all-wise and omniscient, whose creative thought is knowledge itself. **(Mundaka I.1.6–9)**

This is the truth: As from a blazing fire thousands of sparks, similar to it in nature, issue forth, so, O my young friend! manifold beings are produced from the imperishable, and they verily go back to It again. Self-resplendent, formless, unoriginated and pure, that all-pervading Being is both within and without. Anterior both to life and mind. He transcends even the Unmanifested causal state of the universe. From Him are born life, mind, senses, ether, air, fire, water, and earth that supports all. Verily, He is the indwelling spirit within all. Fire is His head; the sun and moon, His eyes; the quarters, His ears; the revelation (the Vedas), His voice; the wind, His breath; the universe, His heart. And from His feet the earth has originated. From Him comes the heaven world, which is the first Fire, having the sun for its fuel; from the moon in the heaven world, the rain-clouds (the second Fire); from the clouds, the herbs on earth (the third Fire). (And from the herbs eaten), man (the fourth Fire) casts the seed in woman (the fifth Fire). In this manner many beings are born of Purusha the all-pervading Being. From His are the Vedic verses, the sacred chants, the sacrificial formulae, preliminary rites, sacrifices, ceremonies, sacrificial gifts, the time of sacrifice, the sacrificer, and the worlds purified by the sun and the moon (which come to one as the fruits of sacrifice). From Him, the gods of various orders, the celestials, men, beasts, birds, in-breath, out-breath, paddy, barley, austerity, faith, truth, continence, and the Law (were born). From Him too, the seven senses in the head, their powers of cognition, their objects and their knowledge, as also the seven seats of sense life traversed by the life-forces centred in the hearts of all creatures. From Him, all the oceans and mountains, from Him, the rivers of every description, from Him, too, all herbs and sap by which the subtle body exists encircled by the gross elements of matter. Verily, that Omnipresent Being is all this—sacrificial works, knowledge and all the rest. O handsome youth! he who knows this supreme, Immortal Being as seated in the cavity of the heart, rends asunder the knot of ignorance even here, in this life. **(Ibid. II.1.1–10)**

This Brahman is the great support—manifesting through all experiences, existing very close, and moving in the cavity of the heart. All that move and breathe and wink are established in It. Know It—the cause of both the gross and the subtle, the adorable of all, the highest of beings, the one above the understanding of creatures. Luminous, subtler than even atoms, that Imperishable Brahman is the abode of the world and all its inhabitants. It is life, speech, mind, reality, immortality. That is the mark which should be penetrated by the mind. Penetrate it, O my friend. **(Ibid. II.2.1,2)**

He is all-wise and all-knowing and His is verily the glory (manifest on earth). In the sky of the heart—the luminous city of Brahman—He is established clothed in mind and guiding life and body. With his seat in the heart, He lives in the whole body of man. By perfect knowledge of Him the wise realize the state of Blissful Immortality. **(Ibid. II.2.7)**

There the sun does not shine, nor the moon and the stars; these lightnings too do not shine—much less this earthly fire! Verily, everything shines, reflecting His glory. This whole world is illumined with His light. Verily, all this is the immortal Brahman! He is everywhere—above, below, in front, at the back, upon the right, upon the left! All this world is indeed the supreme Brahman! **(Ibid. II.2.10,11)**

Vast, divine, beyond all imagination, shines the truth of Brahman. It is subtler than the subtlest, farther than the farthest. It is here within the body, and the sages realize it verily in this life as fixed in the heart. The Self cannot be described by words, nor perceived by the eyes and senses, nor revealed by rituals and penances. When the understanding becomes calm and refined, one's whole being is purified, and then, engaged in meditation, one realizes Him, the Absolute. By means of thought one should know the subtle truth of the Atman within the body, which is permeated by life-force in a fivefold way. Man's thought is interwoven with the senses. When that thought is purified, the Self shines forth. **(Ibid. III.1.7–9)**

For truly, everything is Brahman. And this Self within (Atman) is Brahman. **(Mandukya 2)**

This is the Lord of all—their knower, their inner controller, their source, their origin and dissolution. **(Ibid. 6)**

Brahman is Existence, Intelligence, Infinitude. **(Taittiriya II.1)**

That from which all speech with the mind turns away, not having reached It, knowing the bliss of that Brahman man fears nothing. **(Ibid. II.9)**

The whole world is founded on Prajna and therefore Prajna is Brahman. **(Aitareya III.1)**

Verily, all this universe is Brahman. From Him do all things originate, into Him do they dissolve and by Him are they sustained. On Him should one meditate in tranquillity. For as is one's faith in this world, such one becomes on departing hence. Let one, therefore, cultivate faith. He, who is permeating the mind, who has Prana for his body, whose nature is consciousness, whose resolve is infallible, whose own form is like Akasa, whose creation is all that exists, whose are all the pure desires, who possesses all the agreeable odours and all the pleasant tastes, who exists pervading all this, who is without speech (and other senses), who is free from agitation and eagerness—this my Atman, residing in (the lotus) of the heart—is smaller than a grain of paddy, than a barley corn, than a mustard seed, than a grain of millet. This my Atman residing in (the lotus of) the heart is greater than the earth, greater than the sky, greater than all these worlds. **(Chandogya III.14.1–3)**

'Dear boy, just as through a single clod of clay all that is made of clay would become known, for all modification is but name based upon words and the clay alone is real. Dear boy, just as through a single ingot of gold, all that is made of gold would become known, for all modification is but name based upon words and the gold alone is real. Dear boy, just as through a single nail-parer all that is made of iron would become known, for all modification is but name based upon words and the iron alone is real—such, dear boy, is that teaching.' **(Ibid. VI.1.4–6)**

'In the beginning, dear boy, this was Being alone, one only, without a second. Some say that, in the beginning, this was Non-being alone, one only, without a second. From that Non-being arose Being.' Aruni said, 'But how, indeed, dear boy, could it be so? How could Being arise from Non-being? In truth, dear boy, in the beginning (before creation), there was Being alone, one only, without a second. That Being willed, "May I become many, may I grow forth." It created fire. That fire willed, "May I become many, may I grow forth." It created water. **(Ibid. VII.2.1–3)**

That Being which is this subtle essence (cause), even That all this world has for its self. That is the True. That is the Atman. That thou art, O Svetaketu. **(Ibid. VI.8.7)**

'Just as, dear boy, (some robber) having brought a man from the Gandhara region with his eyes bound up, might leave him in a very desolate place, and just as that man would shout towards the east, or towards the north, or towards the south or towards the west, (saying) "I have been brought here with my eyes bound up, I have been left here with my eyes bound up." And as someone might remove his bandage and tell him, "The Gandhara region is in this direction, proceed in this direction" and as he, enquiring his way from village to village, and being instructed and capable of judging by himself, would reach Gandhara region itself, even so, in this world, the person knows who has a preceptor. And for him, only so long is the delay as he is not liberated (from the body) and then immediately he is merged in the Being. That Being which is this subtle essence, even That all this world has for its self. That is the true. That is the Atman. That thou art, O Svetaketu.' **(Ibid. VI.14.1–3)**

That which is infinite, is alone happiness. There is no happiness in anything finite. The infinite alone is happiness. But one must desire to understand the infinite. **(Ibid. VII.23.1)**

'In which one sees nothing else, hears nothing else, understands nothing else, that is the infinite. But that in which one sees something else, hears something else, understands something else, is the finite. That which is infinite is alone immortal, and that which is finite, is mortal.' 'Revered sir, in what is that infinite established?' 'On its own greatness or not even on its own greatness.' **(Ibid. VII.24.1)**

He should say, 'It (the Brahman called inner Akasa) does not age with the aging of the body, it is not killed by the killing of this. This (Akasa) is the real city of Brahman, in it are contained the desires. This is the Atman, free from evil, free from old age, free from death, free from sorrow, free from hunger, free from thirst, whose desire is of the truth, whose resolve is of the truth. Just as in this world, the subjects follow as they are commanded and whatever province they desire, be it a country or a part of a field, on that they live. **(Ibid. VIII.1.5)**

Now, this Atman is the dyke, the embankment for the safety of these worlds. This dyke, neither the day nor the night crosses, nor old age nor death nor sorrow, nor merit nor demerit. All evils turn back from it, for this Brahman-world is free from evil. **(Ibid. VIII.4.1)**

In the beginning, this universe was verily the self (Viraj) in the form of a person. He pondered and beheld nothing else but himself. He first said, 'I am He'. Therefore he got the name 'I'. Hence even now when anyone is accosted he first says, 'It is I', and then tells the other name that he has. Because he was the first (among the aspirants to the status of Prajapati), and (before) this whole group consumed all evils, therefore he is called Purusha. He who knows thus verily consumes him who wishes to be (Prajapati) in advance of him. (**Brihadaranyaka I.4.1**)

This Self is dearer than a son, dearer than wealth, dearer than all other objects, being nearer (than everything). If anyone (holding the Self as dearest) says to a person describing anything other than the Self as dear, 'What is dear to you will perish', it will certainly be like that, for he is indeed capable of saying so. Therefore one should meditate upon the Self alone as dear . Of him who meditates upon the Self alone as dear, no dear object is short-lived. (**Ibid. I.4.8**)

This (self) was verily Brahman at first. It knew only itself as, 'I am Brahman'. Because of that it became all (the universe). And whosoever among the gods realized it became Brahman. Similarly among the sages, and among men. The sage Vamadeva, realising his own self as That (Brahman), knew, 'I was Manu, and the sun.' And even now whoever knows That in a similar way, viz., as 'I am Brahman', becomes this universe. Even the gods are powerless to prevent his becoming the universe, for he becomes their self. On the other hand, he who adores another god thinking, 'He is different from me, and I am different from Him', does not know. As is an animal (to man), so is he to the gods. As many animals serve a man, so does each man serve the gods. If even one animal is taken away, it causes unpleasantness what should one say of many animals? Therefore it is not pleasant to the gods that men should realize this Self. (**Ibid. I.4.10**)

Brahman has only two forms—gross and subtle, mortal and immortal, limited and unlimited, perceptible and imperceptible. The gross form is that which is other than air and the ether. It is mortal, it is limited, and it is perceptible. The essence of that form which is gross, mortal, limited and perceptible is the shining sun, for it is the essence of those three elements. Now the subtle form—it is air and the ether. It is immortal, it is unlimited, it is imperceptible. The essence of that form which is subtle, immortal, unlimited and imperceptible is the principle that is in the solar orb, for it is the essence of those two elements. This is with reference to the deities. **(Ibid. II.3.1–3)**

'As a lump of salt thrown into water only dissolves into the water, and none can at all pick it up, but from whichever part one takes the water, it has only a saline taste, even so, my dear, this great, endless, infinite Reality is only homogeneous Intelligence. On account of these elements (the self) stands out (separately), and as soon as these are destroyed, (its separate existence) it is also destroyed. After attaining (isolation) it has no (particular) consciousness. This is what I say, my dear', so said Yajnavalkya. **(Ibid. II.4.12)**

This same Self is the ruler of all beings and the king of all beings. Just as all spokes are fixed in the nave and the felloe of a chariot-wheel, even so are all beings, all gods, all worlds, all organs and all these (individuals) selves fixed in this Self. **(Ibid. II.5.15)**

That Brahman is without antecedent and without consequent, without interior and without exterior. This self, which experiences everything, is Brahman. **(Ibid. II.5.19)**

Then Kahola, the son of Kushitaka, questioned him. 'Yajnavalkya', said (He) 'tell me precisely about Brahman that is immediate and indirect—the self that is within all.' 'Which is it that is within all, Yajnavalkya?' 'That which is beyond hunger and thirst, grief and delusion, decrepitude and death. Realising this very Self, Brahmanas give up the desire for sons, for wealth and for worlds, and take up a wandering mendicant's life. Because that which is the desire for sons is the desire for wealth, and that which is the desire for wealth is the desire for worlds, for both these are but desires. Therefore a Brahmana, having mastered Self-knowledge, should seek to live on that strength. Having mastered that strength as well as that knowledge, he becomes meditative; and having mastered both meditativeness and its absence, he becomes a real Brahmana. How does that Brahmana conduct himself? Howsoever he may, he is indeed such. All else but this (state of Brahmanahood) is perishable.' **(Ibid. III.5.1)**

He who dwells in earth but is within it, whom earth does not know, whose body is earth, and who controls earth from within, is the Inner Controller—your own self and immortal. **(Ibid. III.7.3)**

He is never seen, but is the Seer; He is never heard, but is the Hearer; He is never thought of, but is the Thinker; He is never known, but is the Knower. There is no other seer than He, there is no other hearer than He, there is no other thinker than He, there is no other knower than He. He is the Inner Controller—your own Self and immortal. All else but He is perishable. **(Ibid. III. 7.23)**

He said, 'O Gargi, the knowers of Brahman describe It verily as the Absolute. It is neither coarse nor fine, neither short nor long, neither redness nor oiliness, neither shadow nor darkness, neither air nor ether. It is not sticky, nor is it savour or odour. It is without eyes and ears, without the organ of speech and mind, non-effulgent, without the vital force and mouth. It is not a measure, and is devoid of interior or exterior. It does not eat anything, nor does anybody eat it. Under the rule of this very Absolute, O Gargi, the sun and moon are held in their own courses. Under the rule of this very Absolute, O Gargi, heaven and earth hold their own positions. Under the rule of this very Absolute, O Gargi, moments, muhurtas, days and nights, fortnights, months, seasons and years are maintained in their respective places. Under the rule of this Absolute, O Gargi, from the white mountains some rivers flowing eastward, others flowing westward and still others, (flowing in different directions) keep to their respective courses. Under the rule of this very Absolute, O Gargi, people praise the charitable, the gods depend on the sacrificer, and the manes on the detached fire-offering. **(Ibid. III.8.8,9)**

Verily this Absolute, O Gargi, is never seen, but is the Seer; it is never heard, but is the hearer; It is never thought of, but is the Thinker; It is never known, but is the Knower. There is no other seer than It, there is no other hearer than It, there is no other thinker than It, there is no other knower than It. This very Absolute, O Gargi, pervades the unmanifested ether. **(Ibid. III.8.11)**

It is Brahman, which is Absolute Intelligence and Bliss, the ultimate resort of the bestower of wealth, as also of the knower of Brahman who lives in It. **(Ibid. III.9.28)**

'Which is the Self?' 'This (infinite) entity which is reflected in the intellect, which is amid the organs, and which is the (self-effulgent) light within the intellect. Simulating the intellect, it roams between this and the next life; it thinks, as it were, and quivers, as it were. For being one with dreams, it goes beyond this (waking) world, which represents the forms of death (ignorance and its offshoots). **(Ibid. IV.3.7)**

That it does not (apparently) know in that state is because, although (really) knowing in that state, it does not know; for there cannot be any absence of knowing on the part of the knower, since the latter is imperishable. But there is not that second entity differentiated from it which it can know. Where there is a different thing as it were, there one can see another, one can smell another, one can taste another, one can speak to another, one can hear another, one can think about another, one can touch another and one can know another. It becomes (in deep sleep serene) like water, one, the seer and free from duality. This is the world that is Brahman, O Emperor', thus did Yajnavalkya teach Janaka; 'this is its highest goal, this is its highest glory, this is its highest world, this is its highest bliss; all other beings live on a particle of this very bliss. **(Ibid. IV.3.30–32)**

This same self is verily Brahman, as also associated with the intellect, with the mind, with the vital force, with the eyes, with the ears, with earth, with water, with the air, with the ether, with fire and with what is other than fire, with desire and with want of desire, with anger and with the absence of anger, with righteousness and with unrighteousness and with all. Thus it is (proved) that it is associated with what is perceived and with what is inferred. As it does and as it acts, so it becomes: the doer of good becomes good, and the doer of evil becomes evil; it becomes virtuous through a virtuous act and vicious through a vicious act. Others, however, say that the self is identified with desire alone. It resolves as it desires; it does the work that it resolves; and it attains the results of the work it does. **(Ibid. IV.4.5)**

On this theme there is the following Mantra verse: "When all the desires that abide in the intellect of a man have totally left, then the mortal man becomes immortal and realises Brahman in the very body." Just as the lifeless slough of a snake lies cast off in the ant-hill (etc.) even so lies this body. Then the self becomes disembodied and immortal, the Supreme Self, Brahman, the Light of Pure Intelligence. **(Ibid. IV.4.7)**

Brahman is to be known by the mind in accordance with (the instructions of the teacher). There is no diversity whatever in it. He who sees diversity, as it were, in It, goes from death to death. It is to be realized in accordance with (the instructions of a teacher) only as homogeneous, (for) it is unknowable, unchangeable and free from impurities. The Self is superior to the (unmanifested) ether, unborn, infinite and indestructible. That infinite, birthless self (previously described as entity) which is reflected in the intellect and is amid the organs, lies in the Supreme Self that is within the heart. It is the controller of all, the lord of all, the ruler of all. It is not magnified by good work nor degraded in the least by evil work, It is the lord of all, the ruler of beings, the protector of beings. It is the demarcating bank for keeping these worlds distinct from one another. The seekers of Brahman wish to realise It through regular reading of the Vedas, sacrifices, charity and austerity, not leading to death. Knowing It alone one becomes a man of meditation. Seeking this world (of the Self) alone monks give up their homes. (The reason) for this is this: the ancient knowers, it is said, did not desire progeny, thinking, "What shall we do with progeny—we who have realised this world, this Self?"

Giving up the desire for sons, for wealth and for the worlds, they took up a wandering mendicant's life. Since that which is the desire for sons is the desire for wealth, and that which is the desire for wealth is the desire for worlds, for both these are desires. This self is That which has been described as "Not this, not this". This has been stated by this Mantra hymn: "This is the eternal glory of a knower of Brahman, (for) it neither increases nor decreases on account of work. (Hence) one should know the nature of that glory alone. Knowing it one is not affected by evil work". Therefore one who knows as above becomes self-controlled, serene, free from desires, possessed of fortitude and concentrated, and sees the Supreme Self in his own self (body); he sees everything as the Self. Evil does not overtake him; (rather) he goes beyond all evil. Evil does not afflict him; (rather) he burns all evil. He becomes free from evils, desires and doubts, and a Brahmana (a knower of Brahman). This is the world that is Brahman, O Emperor, and you have been helped to It. **(Ibid. IV.4.19–23)**

That infinite, birthless, undecaying, indestructible, immortal and fearless self is Brahman, Brahman is indeed fearless. He who knows (the Self) as above indeed becomes fearless Brahman. **(Ibid. IV.4.25)**

'For, when there is duality, as it were, then one sees another, one smells another, one tastes another, one speaks of another, one hears another, one thinks of another, one touches another, one knows another. But when all has become the very self of the knower of Brahman, then what should one see and through what, what should one smell and through what, what should one taste and through what, what should one hear and through what, what should one think of and through what, what should one touch and through what, what should one know and through what? Through what should one know That because of which all this is known? This self is That which has been described as "Not this, not this". It is imperceptible, for it is not perceived; unshrinking, for it does not shrink; unattached, for It is not attached; untrammelled, It does not suffer, nor perish. Through what, my dear, should one know the Knower? Thus you have been given the instruction, Maitreyi. This much is indeed (the means of) immortality, my dear'. Saying this Yajnavalkya left home. **(Ibid. IV.5.15)**

This being reflected in the mind, radiant by nature, (is realised) in the interior of the heart, like a grain of rice or barley in size. He is the Lord of all, the ruler of all; he rules whatever there is in the universe. **(Ibid. V.6.1)**

In this infinite wheel of Brahman, in which everything lives and rests, the pilgrim soul is whirled about. Knowing the individual soul, hitherto regarded as separate, to be itself the Moving Force, and blessed by Him, it attains immortality. **(Svetasvatara I.6)**

The Lord supports this universe, which consists of a combination of the perishable and the imperishable, the manifest and the unmanifest. As long as the self does not know the Lord, it gets attached to worldly pleasures, and is bound; but when it knows Him, all fetters fall away from it. The conscious subject and the unconcious object, the master and the dependent, are both unborn. She too, who is engaged in bringing about the relation of the enjoyer and the enjoyed (or between these two), is unborn. When all these three are realized as Brahman, the self becomes infinite, universal and free from the sense of agentship. Matter is perishable,but God is imperishabe and immortal. He the only God, rules over the perishable matter and individual souls. By meditating on Him, by uniting with Him, and by becoming one with Him, there is cessation of all illusion in the end. **(Ibid. I.8–10)**

This is to be known as eternally existing in one's own self. Indeed, there is nothing to be known beyond this. As a result of meditation, the enjoyer, the enjoyed and the power which brings about the enjoyment—all are declared to be three aspects of Brahman. **(Ibid. I.12)**

As oil in sesame seeds, as butter in curds, as water in underground springs, as fire in wood, even so this Self is perceived in the self. He who, by means of truthfulness, self-control and concentration, looks again and again for this Self, which is all-pervading like butter contained in milk, and which is rooted in self-knowledge and meditation,—he becomes that Supreme Brahman, the destroyer of ignorance. **(Ibid. I.15,16)**

When the Yogin realizes the truth of Brahman, through the perception of the truth of Atman in this body as a self-luminous entity, then, knowing the Divinity as unborn, eternal and free from all the modifications of Prakriti, he is freed from all sins. This Divinity pervades all directions in their entirety.

He is the first born (Hiranyagarbha). He has entered into the womb. He alone is born, and is to be born in future, He is inside all persons as the Indwelling Self, facing all directions. Salutations to the Divinity who is in the fire, who is in the water, who is in the plants, who is in the trees, who has pervaded the whole universe. **(Ibid. II.15–17)**

It is the self-same One who exists alone at the time of creation and dissolution of the universe, that assumes manifold powers and appears as the Divine Lord by virtue of His inscrutable power of Maya. He it is that protects all the worlds and controls all the various forces working therein. Those who realize this Being become immortal. He who protects and controls the worlds by His own powers, He—Rudra—is indeed one only. There is no one beside Him who can make Him the second. O men, he is present inside the hearts of all beings. After projecting and maintaining all the worlds, He finally withdraws them into Himself. Though God, the creator of heaven and earth, is one only, yet He is the real owner of all the eyes, faces and hands and feet in this universe. It is He who inspires them all to do their respective duties in accordance with the knowledge, past actions and tendencies of the various beings (with whom they appear to be associated). **(Ibid. III.1–3)**

Higher than this Personal Brahman is the infinite Supreme Brahman, who is concealed in all beings according to their bodies, and who, though remaining single, envelops the whole universe. Knowing Him to be the Lord, one becomes immortal. I have realized this great Being who shines effulgent like the sun beyond all darkness. One passes beyond death only on realizing Him. There is no other way of escape from the circle of births and deaths. There is naught higher than or different from Him; naught greater or more minute than Him. Rooted in His own glory He stands like a tree, one without a second and immovable. By that Being the whole universe is filled. That Being is far beyond this world, is formless and free from misery. They who know this become immortal. But all others have indeed to suffer misery alone. Therefore, that Divine Lord, being all-pervading, omnipresent and benevolent, dwells in the hearts of all beings, and makes use of all faces, heads and necks in this world. **(Ibid. III.7–11)**

That Infinite Being has a thousand heads, a thousand eyes and a thousand feet enveloping the whole universe on all sides. He exists beyond ten fingers. That which is, that which was, and that which is yet to be—all this is nothing but this Infinite Being. Though He grows beyond His own nature into the form of the objective universe, He still remains the Lord of immortality. With hands and feet everywhere, with eyes, heads and mouths everywhere, with ears everywhere, That exists, pervading everything in the universe. They realize Him as shining by the functions of all the senses yet without the senses, as the Lord of all, the ruler of all, the refuge of all and the friend of all. **(Ibid. III.14–17)**

Without hands and feet he goes fast and grasps; without eyes He sees; without ears He hears. He knows whatever is to be known, yet there is none who knows Him. They say He is the foremost, the great Infinite Being. Subtler than even the subtlest and greater than the greatest, the Atman is concealed in the heart of the creature. By the grace of the Creator, one becomes free from sorrows and desires, and then realizes Him as the great Lord. I know this undecaying primeval Immanent Self of all, who is omnipresent because of His all-pervasiveness, and whom the expounders of Brahman declare to be eternally free from birth. **(Ibid. III.19–21)**

Thou art the woman, Thou art the man, Thou art the youth and the maiden too. Thou art the old man who totters along, leaning on the staff. Thou art born with faces turned in all directions. Thou art the dark blue butterfly, and the green parrot with red eyes. Though art the thunder-cloud, the seasons and the oceans. Thou art without beginning, and beyond all time and space. Thou art He from whom all the worlds are born. There is a single Female of red, white and black colours, who is unoriginated, and who produces numerous offspring all resembling herself. By her side lies one unborn Male out of attachment for her, while another Male, also unoriginated, forsakes her after having enjoyed her. **(Ibid. IV.3–5)**

Of what avail are the Vedas to him who does not know that indestructible, highest Ethereal Being, in whom the gods and the Vedas reside? Only those who know That are satisfied. **(Ibid. IV.8)**

Know then that Nature is Maya, and that the great God is the Lord of Maya. The whole world is filled with beings who form His parts. One attains infinite peace on realizing that self-effulgent Adorable Lord, the bestower of blessings who, though one, presides over all the various aspects of Prakriti, and in whom this universe dissolves, and in whom it appears in manifold forms. **(Ibid. IV.10–11)**

When ignorance is dispelled, there is neither day nor night, neither being nor non-being. There is only that Auspicious One who is imperishable, and who is worthy of being adored by the creator. From Him has proceeded the ancient wisdom. **(Ibid. IV.18)**

His form does not stand within the range of the senses. No one perceives Him with the eye. Those who know Him through the faculty of intuition as thus seated in their heart, become immortal. **(Ibid. IV.20)**

Ignorance leads to the perishable. Wisdom leads to immortality. Entirely different from these is He, the imperishable, infinite, secret, Supreme Brahman, in whom exists wisdom as well as ignorance, and who governs them both. He alone presides over Nature in all aspects, and controls every form and every cause of production. He witnesses the birth of the first born seer of golden colour and nourishes him with wisdom. **(Ibid. V.1–2)**

Only he who gets attached to the pleasurable qualities of things does work for the sake of its fruits, and enjoys the fruits of his own deeds. Though really the master of the senses, he becomes bound by the three Gunas and assuming various forms, wanders about through the three paths as a result of his own deeds. **(Ibid. V.7)**

That Supreme Divinity who created both Life and Matter who is the source of all arts and sciences, who can be intuited by a pure and devoted mind—realizing Him, the blissful, the incorporeal and the nameless, one is freed from further embodiment. **(Ibid. V.14)**

May we realize Him—the transcendent and adorable master of the universe—who is the supreme Lord over all the lords, the supreme God above all the gods, and the supreme ruler over all the rulers. He has nothing to achieve for Himself, nor has He any organ of action. No one is seen equal or superior to Him. His great power alone is described in the Vedas to be of various kinds, and His knowledge, strength and action are described as inherent in Him. No one in the world is His master, nor has anybody any control over Him. There is no sign by which He can be inferred. He is the cause of all, and the ruler of individual souls. He has no parent, nor is there any one who is His Lord. May the Supreme Being, who spontaneously covers Himself with the products of Nature, just as a spider does with the threads drawn from its own navel, grant us absorption in Brahman! God, who is one only, is hidden in all beings. He is all-pervading, and is the inner self of all creatures. He presides over all actions, and all beings reside in Him. He is the witness, and He is the pure Consciousness free from the three Gunas of Nature. **(Ibid. VI.7–11)**

He is the creator of everything as well as the knower of everything. He is His own source, He is all-knowing, and He is the destroyer of time. He is the repository of all good qualities, and the master of all sciences. He is the controller of Matter and Spirit, and the Lord of the Gunas. He is the cause of liberation from the cycle of birth and death, and of bondage which results in its continuance. **(Ibid. VI.16)**

Though I am birthless, immutable and the Lord of creatures, yet resorting to my Prakriti, I manifest Myself through My own inscrutable power (Maya). Whenever, O descendent of Bharata, righteousness declines and unrighteousness prevails, I manifest Myself. For the protection of the righteous and the destruction of the wicked, and for the establishment of religion, I come into being from age to age. **(Bhagavadgita IV.6–8)**

By whatsoever way men worship Me, even so do I accept them; for in all ways, O Partha, men walk in My path. **(Ibid. IV.11)**

Higher than Myself there is nothing else, O Dhananjaya (Arjuna). In Me all this is strung like gems on a string. **(Ibid. VII.7)**

Not knowing My immutable, unsurpassed supreme nature, the ignorant regard Me the unmanifest, as coming into being. I am not manifest to all, being veiled by My mysterious power (Yoga-maya). This ignorant world does not know Me, the unborn and immutable. I know, O Arjuna, all beings past, present and future, but nobody knows Me. **(Ibid. VII.24–26)**

Beyond this Unmanifest there is another Unmanifest eternal Being that does not perish when all creatures perish. That Unmanifest which is called the Imperishable is said to be the Supreme Goal, attaining which they return not; that is My supreme abode. That Supreme Being, O Partha, in whom are all beings and by whom all this is pervaded, is attainable by one-pointed devotion. **(Ibid. VIII.20–22)**

All this is pervaded by Me of unmanifest form; all beings are in Me but I am not in them. Nor are the beings in Me, behold My divine mystery; (though) the sustainer and the protector of beings, yet, Myself is not in these beings. As the vast wind blowing everywhere ever abides in space, know, even so, do all beings abide in Me. (**Ibid. IX.4–6**)

Neither the gods nor the great sages know My birth; for I am the cause of the gods and the great sages in all respects. (**Ibid. X.2**)

I am, O Gudakesa, the Self residing in the minds of all creatures; I am the beginning, the middle and also the end of beings. (**Ibid. X.20**)

I am also, O Arjuna, that which is the germ of all beings; there is no being, moving or stationary, which can exist without Me. O tormentor of foes, there is no end to My divine glories; these details of My glories I have only stated in brief. Whatever thing is glorious, excellent or pre-eminent, verily, know that is born of a portion of My splendour. But of what avail is it to you to know all these details! I exist pervading this entire universe by a portion of myself. (**Ibid. X.39–42**)

And know the Kshetrajna (embodied self) in all the bodies (Kshetras) to be Myself, O descendant of Bharata. The knowledge of the Kshetra and Kshetrajna (i.e. matter and Spirit) is, in My opinion, true knowledge. (**Ibid. XIII.2**)

I shall tell you that which has to be known, knowing which one attains immortality; it is the beginningless, supreme Brahman, which is said to be neither being nor non-being. With hands and feet everywhere, with eyes, heads and faces everywhere, with ears everywhere, It rests pervading everything in this world. It is manifest in the functions of the various sense-organs, yet bereft of all sense-organs; unattached, yet sustaining everything; without attributes, yet the protector of the qualities. It is without and within all beings, It is moving and unmoving, being subtle, It is incomprehensible, It is far, yet near. It is undivided in beings and yet remains as if divided; that Knowable is the sustainer of beings as also the destroyer and creator. It is the light of lights and is said to be beyond all darkness. It is knowledge, the knowable and accessible through knowledge, and is implanted in the heart of all beings. **(Ibid. XIII.12–17)**

This supreme Self, being without a beginning and devoid of attributes, is immutable. Though residing in the body, O son of Kunti, It neither acts nor is It attached. **(Ibid. XIII.31)**

Whatever forms, O sor. of Kunti, are born in different wombs, of them the great Nature is the womb, and I am the seed-giving father. **(Ibid. XIV.4)**

The light in the sun which illumines the world and that in the moon and the fire—know that light to be Mine. Entering the earth with My energy, I support the beings; and I nourish all the herbs, becoming the watery moon. Residing in the bodies of beings as the digestive fire (Vaisvanara), and united with Prana and Apana (breaths), I digest the four kinds of food. I am seated in the heart of all beings. From Me are memory and knowledge as also their loss. I alone am to be known through all the Vedas, I am the originator of the Vedantic tradition, and I am also the knower of the Vedas. **(Ibid. XV.12–15)**

Different from these is the Supreme Being known as the Supreme Self (Paramatman) the immutable Lord, who having entered the three worlds sustains them. Since I am beyond the perishable and even excel the imperishable, therefore I am well-known in this world and in the Vedas as the supreme Being. (Purushottama). **(Ibid. XV.17,18)**

In the heart of all beings, O Arjuna, resides the Lord, whirling all of them by His Maya as if they were mounted on a machine. **(Ibid. XVIII.61)**

SOUL

The Self is one. Unmoving, It is faster than the mind. Having preceded the mind, It is beyond the reach of the senses. Ever steady, It outstrips all that run. By Its mere presence, it enables the cosmic energy to sustain the activities of living-beings. It moves, and It moves not. It is far, and It is near. It is within all this, and it is also outside all this. **(Isa 4,5)**

It is the Atman, the Spirit, by whose power the ear hears, the eye sees, the tongue speaks, the mind understands and life functions. The wise man separates the Atman from these faculties, rises out of sense-life and attains immortality. **(Kena I.2)**

That is surely different from the known, and It is beyond the unknown. Thus we have heard from the ancients who expounded It to us. **(Ibid. I.4)**

This (Atman) can never be well comprehended, if taught by an inferior person, even though often pondered upon. Unless it is taught by another, there is no (other) way to it. Subtler than the subtlest, it is unarguable. **(Katha I.2.8)**

The knowing soul is not born, nor does it die. It has not come into being from anything, nor anything has come into being from it. This unborn, eternal, everlasting, ancient One suffers no destruction, even when the body is being destroyed. If the killer thinks that he is killing, and the killed thinks he is killed, both of them know it not. It kills not, nor is it killed. Atman, smaller than the smallest and greater than the greatest, dwells in the hearts of creatures. The desireless onc being free from grief, realises that glory of Atman through purity of senses and mind. Though sitting still, He travels far; though lying down, He goes everywhere. Who can know besides me, that effulgent Being who rejoices and rejoices not? The wise one does not grieve, having known the bodiless, all-pervading supreme Atman who dwells in (all) impermanent bodies. This Atman cannot be attained by the study of the Vedas, nor by intellect, nor even by much learning; by him it is attained whom it chooses,—this, his (own) Atman, reveals its own (real) form. **(Ibid. I.2.18–23)**

The Atman, hidden in all beings reveals (itself) not (to all) but is seen (only) by the seers of the subtle through their pointed and subtle intellect. **(Ibid. I.3.12)**

Having realised that (Atman) which is soundless, touchless, formless, imperishable, and also without taste and smell, eternal, without beginning or end, even beyond the Mahat, immutable,—one is released from the jaws of death. **(Ibid. I.3.15)**

That Atman by which man cognizes light, tastes, smells, sounds, touches and the sexual contacts, what is there unknowable to that Atman in this world? The wise man grieves not, having realised that great, all-pervading Atman through which one perceives, all objects in dream as well as in the waking state. He who knows this Atman, the enjoyer of honey, the sustainer of life and the lord of the past and the future, as very near,—he fears no more hereafter. He who was born of knowledge in the beginning, and born (even) prior to the waters,—(one) who sees him as dwelling with the elements, having entered the heart, (he verily sees Brahman). **(Ibid. II.1.3–6)**

That from which the sun rises and into which it merges again,—in that are all the gods fixed, and none can verily transcend it. **(Ibid. II.1.9)**

As pure water poured into pure water becomes the same, so O Gautama, becomes the self of the sage who knows (the unity of the Atman). **(Ibid. II.1.15)**

As one fire, having entered the world, assumes forms

according to the shapes of the different objects (it burns), so the one Atman that exists in all the beings appears in (different) forms according to the different objects (it enters); and it (exists) also beyond them. As one air, having come into the world, assumes (different) forms according to the different objects (it enters as breath), so the one Atman that abides in the heart of all beings appears in different forms according to the different objects (it enters); and it (exists) also beyond them. As the sun, the eye of the whole world, is not contaminated by the external ocular impurities, so being beyond the world, the one Atman that resides in all beings is never touched by the miseries of the world. (That) one (supreme) Ruler, the soul of all beings, who makes His one form manifold, —those wise men who perceive Him as existing in their own self, to them belongs eternal happiness and to none else. He, the eternal among non-eternals, the intelligence in the intelligent, who, though One, fulfils the desires of many,—those wise men who perceive Him as existing within their own self, to them belongs eternal peace, and to none else. **(Ibid. II.2.9–13)**

The Purusha of the size of a thumb, the inner soul, dwells always in the heart of beings. One should separate him from the body as the central stalk from the rush grass. Know him to be the pure, the immortal, yea, the pure, the immortal. **(Ibid. II.3.17)**

Two birds, bound one to the other in close friendship, perch on the self-same tree. One of them eats the fruits of the tree with relish, while the other looks on without eating. Seated on the self-same tree, one of them, the personal self, sunken in ignorance and deluded, grieves for his impotence. But when he sees the Other—the Lord, the Worshipful—as also His glory, he becomes free from dejection. When the seer realizes the self-effulgent Being—ruler, maker and source of the creator even—then that wise one, shaking off merits and demerits, becomes stainless, and attains supreme Unity. **(Mundaka III.1.1–3)**

The Self is not attained through discourses, nor through intellectuality, nor through much learning. It is gained only by him who longs for It with the whole heart. For to such a one the Self reveals Its own nature. The self is not gained by men of weak spirit, nor by the careless, nor by those practising improper austerities. But wise men who strive with vigour, attention and propriety, attain union with Brhaman. The sages who have attained the Self, find satisfaction in wisdom (and long for nothing else); they are perfected in soul, non-attached and tranquil. Having realized the all-pervading Spirit everywhere, those wise and devout ones enter into the all. **(Ibid. III.2.3–5)**

The Fourth (Turiya), the wise say, is not inwardly cognitive, nor outwardly cognitive, nor cognitive both-wise, neither is it an indefinite mass of cognition, nor collective cognition, nor non-cognition. It is unseen, unrelated, inconceivable, uninferable, unimaginable, indescribable. It is the essence of the one self-cognition common to all states of consciousness. All phenomena cease in it. It is peace, it is bliss, it is non-duality. This is the Self, and it is to be realised. **(Mandukya 7)**

As a spider moves along the thread (it produces), or as from a fire little sparks scatter, just so from this Self issue all organs, all worlds, all gods and all living beings. Its secret name is the Truth of truth. The vital force is truth and It is the Truth of that. **(Brihadaranyaka II.1.20)**

Yajnavalkya said, 'Verily the husband is dear (to the wife) not for the sake of the husband, my dear, but it is for her own sake that he is dear. Verily the wife is dear (to the husband) not for the sake of the wife, my dear, but it is for his own sake that she is dear. Verily sons are dear (to parents) not for the sake of the sons, my dear, but it is for the sake of the parents themselves that they are dear. Verily wealth is dear not for the sake of the wealth, my dear, but it is for one's own sake that it is dear. Verily the Brahmana is dear not for the sake of the Brahmana, my dear, but it is for one's own sake that he is dear. Verily the Kshatriya is dear not for the sake of the Kshatriya, my dear, but it is for ones's own sake that he is dear. Verily worlds are dear not for the sake of the worlds, my dear, but it is for one's own sake that they are dear. Verily the gods are dear not for the sake of the gods, my dear, but it is for one's own sake that they are dear. Verily beings are dear not for the sake of beings, my dear, but it is for one's own sake that they are dear. Verily all is dear not for the sake of all, my dear, but it is for one's own sake that all is dear. The Self, my dear Maitreyi, should verily be realised: should be heard of, reflected on and meditated upon. By the realisation of the Self alone, my dear, through hearing, reflection and meditation all this is known. **(Ibid. II.4.5)**

This Self is indeed the mighty Lord. He is the imperishable (internal) light that controls everything. He guides the intellect of all beings so as to enable them to gain that extremely pure statre (of Mukti). **(Svetasvatara III.12)**

It is He who resides in the body, the city of nine gates. He is the soul that sports in the outside world. He is the master of the whole world, animate and inanimate. **(Ibid. III.18)**

Two birds of beautiful plumage, who are inseparable friends, reside on the self-same tree. Of these, one eats the fruits of the tree with relish while the other looks on without eating. Sitting on the same tree the individual soul gets entangled and feels miserable, being deluded on account of his forgetting his divine nature. When he sees the other, the Lord of all, whom all devotees worship, and realizes that all greatness is His, then he is relieved of his misery. **(Ibid. IV.67)**

This Divinity, who created the universe and who pervades

everything, always dwells in the hearts of creatures, being finitized by emotions, intellect, will and imagination. Those who realize this become immortal. (**Ibid. IV.17**)

It (self) is not born and it does not die at any time. And it does not again come into existence by being born. It (self) is birthless, constant, eternal and ancient; it is not slain when the body is slain. (**Bhagavadgita II.20**)

Just as a person gives up worn out clothes and puts on other new ones, even so does the embodied self give up decrepit bodies and enter other new ones. Weapons do not cut it, fire does not burn it, water also does not moisten it, and wind does not dry it. This (self) is indeed incapable of being cut, incombustible, incapable of being moistened and of being dried; it is eternal, all-pervading, stable, immovable, and primordial. (**Ibid. II.22–24**)

The supreme Purusha in this body is called the Onlooker, the Permitter, the Nourisher, the Protector, the great Lord, and also the supreme Self. (**Ibid. XIII.22**)

Verily, a part of Myself, having become this eternal embodied soul, draws to this world of beings the senses with the mind as the sixth, which rest in Nature (Prakriti). (**Ibid. XV.7**)

SPIRITUAL PRACTICE

He understands It, who conceives It not, and he understands It not, who conceives It. It is the unknown to the man of true knowledge, but to the ignorant It is the 'Known'. Indeed, he attains immortality, who intuits It in and through every modification of the mind. Through the Atman he obtains real strength, and through knowledge, immortality. If one has realised It here in this world, then there is true life; if he has not realised here, great is the destruction. Discerning the Atman in every single being, the wise man rises from sense-life, and attains immortality. **(Kena II.3–5)**

Austerity, restraint, dedicated work—these are the foundations of it (the saving knowledge of the Upanishads). The Vedas are all its limbs. Truth is its abode. **(Ibid. IV.8)**

Whatever there is changeful in this ephemeral world,—all that must be enveloped by the Lord. By this renunciation (of the world), support yourself. Do not covet the wealth of anyone. **(Isa 1)**

The wise man who perceives all beings as not distinct from his own Self at all, and his own Self as the Self of every being—he does not, by virtue of that perception, hate any one. What delusion, what sorrow is there for the wise man who sees the unity of existence and perceives all beings as his own Self? **(Ibid. 7)**

One thing is the good and (quite) different indeed is the pleasant; having been of different requisitions, they both bind the Purusha. Good befalls him who follows the good, but loses he the goal, who chooses the pleasant. Both the good and the pleasant approach man; the wise one discriminates the two, having examined them well. Yea, the wise man prefers the good to the pleasant, but the fool chooses the pleasant, through avarice and attachment. **(Katha I.2.1,2)**

This (Atman) can never be well comprehended, if taught by an inferior person, even though often pondered upon. Unless it is taught by another, there is no (other) way to it. Subtler than the subtlest, it is unarguable. **(Ibid. I.2.8)**

This Atman cannot be attained by the study of the Vedas, nor by intellect, nor even by much learning; by him it is attained whom it chooses,—this, his (own) Atman, reveals its own (real) form. Neither those who have not refrained from wickedness, nor the unrestrained, nor the unmeditative; nor one with unpacified mind, can attain this even by knowledge. **(Ibid. I.2.23–24)**

Know that the soul is the master of the chariot, who sits within it, and the body is the chariot. Consider the intellect as the charioteer, and the mind as the rein. The senses, they say, are the horses, and their roads are the sense-objects. The wise call Him the enjoyer (when He is) united with the body, the senses and the mind. If one is always of unrestrained mind and devoid of right understanding, his senses become uncontrollable like the wicked horses of a charioteer. But he who is always of restrained mind and has right understanding, his senses are controllable like the good horses of a charioteer. And he who is devoid of proper understanding, thoughtless and always impure, never attains that goal, and gets into the round of births and deaths. But he who is intelligent, ever pure and with mind controlled, verily reaches that goal whence none is born again. The man who has intelligence for His charioteer and the mind as the (well-controlled) rein, he attains the end of the journey, that supreme place of Vishnu. **(Ibid. I.3.3–9)**

Arise, awake, (O man)! Realize (that Atman) having approached the excellent (teachers). Like the sharp edge of a razor is that path, difficult to cross and hard to tread,—so say the wise. **(Ibid. I.3.14)**

The self-existent (god) has rendered the senses (so) defective that they go outward, and hence man sees the external and not the internal self. (Only, perchance) some wise man desirous of immortality turns his eyes in, and beholds the inner Atman. Children pursue the external pleasures (and so) they fall into the snare of the wide-spread death. But the wise do not desire (anything) in this world, having known what is eternally immortal in the midst of all non-eternals. **(Ibid. II.1.1,2)**

The Prana, being present, the whole universe comes out of Him and vibrates within Him. He is a great terror like the raised thunderbolt. Those who know this become immortal.

For fear of Him the fire burns; for fear of Him shines the sun; for fear of Him do Indra, Vayu and Death, the fifth, proceed (with their respective functions). **(Ibid. II.3.3)**

When the five senses of perception lie still with the mind (in the self) when even the intellect works not,—that is the supreme state, they say. That firm control of the senses is known as Yoga. Then the Yogin becomes free from all vagaries of the mind; for the Yoga can be acquired and lost. **(Ibid. II.3.10–11)**

When all the desires that dwell in the heart are destroyed, then the mortal becomes immortal, and he attains Brahman even here. When here in this body all knots of the heart are rent asunder, the mortal becomes immortal—so far is the instruction (of all Vedanta). **(Ibid. II.3.14,15)**

Taking as bow the mighty weapon furnished by the Upanishads, fix on it the arrow rendered sharp by constant meditation. And having drawn it with the mind absorbed in His thought, penetrate that mark—the imperishable Brahman. Om—the mystic syllable—is the bow; the self within, the arrow; and Brhman, the target. One should hit that mark with an undistracted mind, and like the arrow, become one with it. He in whom the heaven, the earth and the interspace are centred, together with the mind and all life-breaths (Pranas),—know Him alone as the one Self of all, and desist from all other talk. This is the man's bridge to the shore of Immortality (across the ocean of life). **(Mundaka II.2.3–5)**

When a person realizes Him in both the high and thc low, the knots of his heart are loosened, his doubts dispelled, and his Karmas, exhausted. **(Ibid. II.2.8)**

The Self is attained through veracity, concentration, wisdom and continence, all constantly cultivated. When impurities dwindle (thus), the ascetics behold Him—stainless, resplendent —within the very body. Only the truthful win, not the untruthful. By truth is laid out the 'divine path', along which the sages, free from desires ascend to the supreme abode of the True. **(Ibid. III.1.5,6)**

The Self cannot be described by words, nor perceived by the eyes, and the senses, nor revealed by rituals and penances. When the understanding becomes calm and refined, one's whole being is purified, and then, engaged in meditation, one realizes Him, the Absolute. **(Ibid. III.1.8)**

As rivers, flowing, disappear in the ocean, losing name and form, so the wise man, free from name and form, goes unto the highest of the high—the Supreme Divinity. **(Ibid. III.2.8)**

Only when man shall roll up the sky like a skin, will there be an end of misery for them without realizing God. **(Svetasvatara VI.20)**

These truths, when taught, shine forth only in that high-souled one who has supreme devotion to God, and an equal degree of devotion to the spiritual teacher. They shine forth in that high-souled one only. **(Ibid. VI.23)**

To work alone you have the right, but never claim its results. Let not the results of actions be your motive, nor be attached to inaction. Established in Yoga, O Dhananjaya (Arjuna), perform actions, giving up attachment, and unconcerned as to success or failure; (this) equanimity is called Yoga. **(Gita II.47,48)**

When a man gives up all desires of the mind, O Partha, and himself delights in his Self, then he is said to be a 'man of steady wisdom'. He who is unperturbed in misery and free from desires amidst pleasures, who is devoid of all attachments, fear and anger—that sage is said to be of steady wisdom. He who is free from affection everywhere, and who getting whatever good or evil, neither welcomes nor hates them has steady wisdom. And when he completely withdraws his senses from the sense-objects, even as a tortoise its limbs, (then) his wisdom is steady. **(Ibid. II.55–58)**

But that person of controlled self who moves about amidst sense-objects with the senses governed by the self and free from attachment and aversion,—he attains serenity. **(Ibid. II.64)**

He attains peace into whom all sense-objects enter, even as rivers enter an ocean which is unaffected though being ever filled, and not one who is desirous of enjoyments. That person who is giving up all sense-objects goes about unattached, devoid of the idea of ownership and free from egoism—he attains peace. **(Ibid. II.70,71)**

By this (sacrifice) entertain the gods and let the gods entertain you; entertaining each other you will both attain supreme good. **(Ibid. III.11)**

Therefore always perform action which has to be done, unattached; verily, man attains the highest by performing action unattached. **(Ibid. III.19)**

The wise man should not unsettle the faith of the ignorant who are attached to work. He should make them devoted to all work, performing action himself intently. **(Ibid. III.26)**

Renouncing all actions in Me with your mind resting on the Self, and giving up hope and idea of ownership, fight, being free from fever. **(Ibid. III.30)**

In respect of each of the senses, attachments and aversions to objects are fixed. One should not come under their sway, for they are impediments in one's way. **(Ibid. III.34)**

Therefore, controlling the senses at the very outset, O best of the Bharatas (Arjuna), kill this sinful thing which destroys realization and knowledge. **(Ibid. III.41)**

He who sees inaction in action and action in inaction is wise amongst men; he is poised and a performer of all actions. **(Ibid. IV.18)**

The sacrifice through knowledge is superior to sacrifices performed with materials, O scorcher of foes; all actions in their entirety, O Partha, are comprised in knowledge. **(Ibid. IV.33)**

The man of faith, zeal, and self control attains knowledge; having attained knowledge, he immediately attains supreme Peace. He who is ignorant, wanting in faith, and of a doubting mind is ruined; for the doubting man there is neither this nor the other world, nor happiness. **(Ibid. IV.39,40)**

He who performs actions dedicating them to the Lord and giving up attachments is not touched by sin, as a lotus leaf by water. **(Ibid. V.10)**

But those whose ignorance has been destroyed by the knowledge of the Self—their knowledge, like the sun, manifests that highest Being. **(Ibid. V.16)**

The knower of Brahman who is established in Brahman, poised in mind and undeluded, is not elated on getting what is pleasant nor feels worried on getting what is unpleasant. **(Ibid. V.20)**

Shutting out external sense-objects, fixing the gaze between the eye-brows, controlling the outgoing and incoming breaths that move through the nostrils with the senses, mind and intellect restrained, and free from desire, fear and anger, the sage who has Liberation as his highest goal is indeed ever free. **(Ibid. V.27–28)**

For the sage who desires to attain to Yoga, action is said to be the means; and for him alone, when he has attained to Yoga, inaction is said to be the means. **(Ibid. VI.3)**

One should raise oneself through the self, and never lower oneself; for the self alone is one's friend and the self alone is one's enemy. To him who has conquered the self (body and senses) by his self, the self is his friend; for the uncontrolled man, however, the self alone is adverse like an enemy. **(Ibid. VI.5,6)**

The Yogi, with his mind and self (body) subjugated, free from desire, destitute, and living alone in solitude, should constantly concentrate his mind. In a clean spot fixing his seat firm, neither too high nor too low, made of the Kusa grass, skin and cloth one on top of the other—sitting on that, with the activities of the mind and the senses controlled, concentrating his mind, he should practise Yoga for the purification of the mind. **(Ibid. VI.10–12)**

Holding the trunk, head and neck erect and steady, becoming firm, fixing the gaze on the tip of his nose and not looking around, tranquil in mind, fearless, practising continence, controlling the mind, intent on he should sit absorbed having Me as the supreme goal. Thus constantly concentrating the mind, the Yogi, with his mind controlled, attains the peace culminating in final Beatitude in the form of abiding in Me. **(Ibid. VI.13-15)**

Having completely renounced all desires born of fancy, controlling well the senses from all sides by the mind alone, (Yoga should be practised). One should withdraw by degrees establishing the mind in the Self by the intellect regulated by concentration, and should not think of anything else. **(Ibid. VI.24–25)**

The man whose mind is absorbed through Yoga and who sees the same (Brahman) everywhere, sees the Self in all beings and all beings in the Self. He who sees Me everywhere and sees all things in Me, does not lose sight of Me, nor do I of him. He who worships me residing in all beings in a spirit of unity, becomes a Yogi and, whatever his mode of life, lives in Me. He who by comparison with himself looks upon the pleasure and pain in all creatures as similar—that Yogi, O Arjuna, is considered the best. **(Ibid. VI.29–32)**

He who at the time of death remembers Me alone and passes out, leaving the body, attains My being—there is no doubt about this. **(Ibid. VIII.5)**

Therefore, remember Me at all times and fight; with your mind and intellect devoted to Me, you shall attain Me alone, there is no doubt about this. **(Ibid. VIII.7)**

Controlling all the inlets (organs), confining the mind to the heart, fixing the life-breath in the head, betaking himself to absorption in Yoga, repeating the monosyllable Om, which is Brahmân, and thinking of Me, he who departs leaving the body, attains the highest Goal. **(Ibid. VIII.12–13)**

Those persons, who think of nothing else and worship Me through meditation—the accession to and the maintenance of the welfare of such ever-devout persons I look after. Even those devotees of other gods who worship (them) endowed with faith, worship Me alone, O son of Kunti (Arjuna), though in an unauthorized way. I am the enjoyer, and the lord also, of all sacrifices. But they do not know Me in truth; therefore they fall down. The worshippers of the gods go to the gods, the worshippers of the manes go to the manes, the worshippers of the spirits go to the spirits, and My worshippers come to Me. He who with devotion offers Me a leaf, a flower, a fruit or water, that devout offering of the pure-minded one I accept. Whatever you do, or eat, or sacrifice, or give, whatever austerity you perform, that, O son of Kunti, offer unto Me. Thus you will be rid of the bonds of action resulting in good and evil; being free and with your mind endowed with the Yoga of renunciation, you will attain Me. I am the same to all beings; there is no one hateful or dear to Me; but they who worship

Me with devotion, are in Me, and I am also in them. (**Ibid. IX.22–29**)

Fix your mind on Me, be My devotee, sacrifice to Me and bow down to Me; thus fixing the mind on Me and having Me for the supreme goal, you will attain Me alone. (**Ibid. IX.34**)

He who works for Me, has Me for the supreme goal, is devoted to Me, and non-attached, and bears no hatred towards any creature, he attains to Me, O Pandava. (**Ibid. XI.55**)

Those who worship Me fixing their mind on Me, ever devoted, and endowed with supreme faith—them I regard as the best Yogins. But they who worship the Imperishable, Indecribable, Unmanifest, All-pervading, Inconceivable, Changeless, Immovable and Eternal, controlling well their senses, even-minded everywhere and devoted to the good of all beings, (also) attain Me alone. (**Ibid. XII.24**)

Non-envious, friendly, and compassionate towards all beings, free from ideas of possession and ego consciousness, sympathetic in pain and pleasures, forgiving, always contended, contemplative, self-controlled, of firm conviction with his mind and intellect dedicated to Me—such a devotee of Mine is dear to Me. From whom the world gets no trouble, and who gets no trouble from the world, who is free from elation, jealousy, fear and anxiety—he is dear to Me. Independent, clean, dexterous, indifferent, untroubled, and discarding all endeavours—such a devotee of Mine is dear to Me. He who neither rejoices nor dislikes nor grieves nor desires, who renounces good and evil, and who is devoted, is dear to Me. Alike to foe and friend, in honour and dishonour, in heat and cold, happiness and misery, free from attachment, alike in praise and censure, reticent, satisfied with anything, without a home, steady in mind— such a devoted person is dear to Me. Those devotees who practise this nectar-like religion just taught with faith, and with Me as their supreme goal, are extremely dear to Me. **(Ibid. XII.13–20)**

Humility, unostentatiousness, harmlessness, forbearance, uprightness, service of the Guru, purity, steadiness, self-control, dispassion for sense-objects and absence of egoism, seeing misery and evil in birth, death, old age and sickness, non-attachment and non-identification with son, wife, home, etc., always being even-minded whether good or evil befalls, unswerving devotion to Me through the Yoga of non-separation, resorting to solitude, and aversion for company, always being devoted to spiritual knowledge, perception of the aim of the knowledge of Truth—all this is called knowledge. What is different from this is ignorance. **(Ibid. XIII.7–11)**

Some see the Self in the Self by the self through meditation, others by (the path of) knowledge, some others by Yoga and (still) others by the path of action. Others (again), not knowing thus, worship by hearing from others; verily, they also, being devoted to hearing, go beyond death. **(Ibid. XIII.24–25)**

He who sees the supreme Lord abiding equally in all beings, the imperishable amidst the perishable—he sees indeed. For, seeing the Lord abiding equally everywhere, he does not injure the Self by the self; therefore he attains the supreme goal. **(Ibid. XIII.27,28)**

I shall tell you again the supreme knowledge—the best of all knowledged, knowing which all the sages have attained supreme felicity from hence. By resorting to this knowledge they, having attained to My nature, are not reborn even at the time of creation nor are they distressed at the time of dissolution. The great Nature is My womb; in that I place the germ, and from that, O descendent of Bharata, is the origin of all beings. **(Ibid. XIV.1–3)**

By what characteristics, O Lord, is one who has transcended these three Gunas known? What is his conduct, and how does he transcend these three Gunas? He who does not hate when the light (of knowledge), activity and delusion arise, O son of Pandu, nor desires them when they cease; He who rests like one indifferent and is not disturbed by the Gunas, who, realizing that the Gunas alone function, is steady and does not waver; alike in pleasure and pain, Self-abiding, regarding a clod of earth, a stone and gold as of equal worth, the same towards agreeable and disagreeable objects, calm and the same to praise and blame bestowed on him; the same in honour and dishonour, the same towards friend and foe, habituated to renounce all actions—such a person is said to have transcended the Gunas. He who serves Me alone through the unswerving Yoga of devotion, transcends these Gunas and becomes fit for the state of Brahman. For I am the embodiment of Brahman, of immutable immortality, of the eternal religion and of absolute bliss. **(Ibid. XIV.21–28)**

Fearlessness, purity of heart, steadfastness in the Yoga of knowledge, charity, self-control, sacrifice, study of the Vedas, austerity, uprightness, non-injury, truthfulness, absence of anger, self-sacrifice, tranquility, freedom from slander, kindness to beings, non-covetousness, gentleness, modesty, absence of fickleness, boldness, forgiveness, fortitude, purity, absence of hatred, absence of conceit,—these belong to one born for divine wealth, O descendent of Bharata. **(Ibid. XVI.1–3)**

There are three types of gates to hell destructive of the self-lust, anger and greed; therefore these three should be shunned. The man who has got rid of these three gates to darkness, O son of Kunti, practises what is good for himself, and thus goes to the supreme Goal. He who, setting aside the ordinances of the scriptures, acts under the impulse of desire, attains neither perfection nor happiness nor the supreme Goal. So let the Scriptures be your authority in ascertaining what ought to be done and what ought not to be done. Having known what has been prescribed by the Scriptures, you should act in this matter. **(Ibid. XVI.21–24)**

These men who practise severe austerities not enjoined by the Scriptures, being given to ostentation and self-conceit possessed of desire, attachment and pertinacity, and senseless, torture the elements in the body, as also Me residing within it—know them to be of demoniac resolves. **(Ibid. XVII.5–6)**

Work in the form of sacrifice, gift and austerity should not be relinquished, but should indeed be performed; (for) sacrifice, gift and austerity are sanctifying to the wise. But even these activities should be performed giving up attachment and fruit—this is My decided and best view. **(Ibid. XVIII.5–6)**

From whom proceeds the activity of all beings, and by whom all this is pervaded—worshipping Him through his own duty a man attains perfection. Better is one's own duty, though defective, than the duty of another, well performed. Doing the duty ordained by one's own nature, one incurs no sin. One should not, O sôn of Kunti, relinquish the duty to which one is born, although it may be attended with evil; for all undertakings are covered by defect, as fire by smoke. He whose understanding is unattached everywhere, whose mind is conquered, who is bereft of desires, attains by renunciation that supreme state of freedom from action. **(Ibid. XVIII.46–49)**

Endued with a pure understanding, controlling the mind with tenacity, relinquishing sense-objects such as sound, and laying aside likes and dislikes; resorting to a sequestered place, eating little, controlled in speech, body and mind, always devoted to the Yoga of contemplation, cultivating dispassion; forsaking egotism, power, arrogance, desire, anger and superfluous things, free from the notion of 'mine' and tranquil, he is fit for becoming Brahman. Becoming Brahman and tranquil-minded, he neither grieves nor desires; alike to all beings, he attains supreme devotion to Me. By devotion he knows me truly, how much and what I am, Then having known Me truly, he forthwith enters into Me. **(Ibid. XVIII.51–58)**

Take refuge in Him alone with all your heart, O descendent of Bharata (Arjuna); by His grace you shall attain supreme peace and the eternal abode. **(Ibid. XVIII.62)**

Fix your mind on Me, be devoted to Me, worship Me, and bow down to Me; then you shall come to Me. Truly do I promise you, for you are dear to Me. Giving up all duties, take refuge in Me alone. I will liberate you from all sins. Do not grieve. **(Ibid. XVIII.65,66)**